Lingo

A language spotter's guide to Europe

Gaston Dorren

....

With contributions by
Jenny Audring, Frauke Watson
and Alison Edwards (translation)

P

PROFILE BOOKS

This paperback edition published in 2015

First published in Great Britain in 2014 by
Profile Books, 3 Holford Yard
Bevin Way
London WC1X 9HD
www.profilebooks.com

1 3 5 7 9 10 8 6 4 2

Printed and bound in Great Britain by
CPI Group (UK) Ltd, Croydon CR0 4YY

Typeset in Gentium to a design by Henry Iles.

This book was published with the support of the
Dutch Foundation for Literature.

N **ederlands**
letterenfonds
dutch foundation
for literature

ISBN 978 1 78125 417 2
e-ISBN 978 1 78283 139 6

Mixed Sources
Product group from well-managed
forests and other controlled sources
www.fsc.org Cert no. TT-COC-002227
© 1996 Forest Stewardship Council

'*Lingo* is that rare thing: a book about language that manages to be both genuinely interesting and enormous fun ... a book that brims with joy at linguistic variety and invention' *Sunday Telegraph*

'An entertaining, accessible guide ... [*Lingo*] tells us an impressive amount about Europe' *Financial Times*

'Entertaining even for the most determinedly monoglot of travellers' *Telegraph*

'A new approach to understanding the world ... ideal for any cunning linguist' *Wanderlust*

'Full of charm and pleasing detail ... [an] amusing tour of Europe's linguistic landscape' *Spectator*

'Full of odd linguistic facts ... fascinating' *Times Literary Supplement*

'An amiable and entertaining examination of European languages in all their idiosyncratic glory.' *Belfast Telegraph*

'[One of those] books one remembers long after one has read them.' *Scotsman*

'A detailed tour of 50-odd European languages and dialects ... *Lingo* [is a] book to dip into as much as to read cover to cover.' *Sydney Morning Herald*

'Witty and informative, with a wealth of engaging comments on all things language-related on our continent ... highly amusing' *Morning Star*

GASTON DORREN is a linguist, journalist and polyglot. He speaks Dutch, Limburgish, English, German, French and Spanish, and reads Afrikaans, Esperanto, Frisian, Portuguese, Italian, Catalan, Danish, Norwegian, Swedish and Luxembourgish. He is the author of two books in Dutch – *Nieuwe tongen* (New Tongues) on the languages of migrants, and *Taaltoerisme* (Language Tourism), on which *Lingo* is based – and an app, the *Language Lover's Guide to Europe*. When not writing, he likes to perform songs – in several languages, of course. Gaston lives with his wife in Amersfoort, the Netherlands.

gastondorren.com
languageloversguide.com

'Two languages in one head? No one can live at that speed! Good Lord, man, you're asking the impossible.' 'But the Dutch speak four languages and they smoke marijuana.' 'Yes, but that's cheating'.

Eddie Izzard, *Dress to Kill*

Contents

Introduction

PART ONE Next of tongue

Languages and their families

PART TWO Past perfect discontinuous

Languages and their history

PART THREE War and peace

Languages and politics

PART FOUR Werds, wirds, wurds ...

Written and spoken

PART FIVE Nuts and bolts

Languages and their vocabulary

PART SIX Talking by the book

Languages and their grammar

PART SEVEN Intensive care

Languages on the brink and beyond

PART EIGHT Movers and shakers

Linguists who left their mark

PART NINE Warts and all

Linguistic portrait studies

*

Introduction

What Europeans speak

The attitude of English speakers to foreign languages can be summed up thus: let's plunder, not learn them. A huge proportion of English vocabulary is of French, Latin or otherwise non-native origin. But the natives have never had much of a taste for acquiring a foreign language in its entirety. 'Anything short of speaking the language I shall be delighted to undertake', Dickens had Mr Meagles say in *Little Dorrit*, while a century and a half later, British comedian Eddie Izzard explains his country's monolinguals: 'Two languages in one head? No one can live at that speed.'

These are caricatures, of course, but the British passion for language, though intense, generally takes form in a somewhat exclusive fascination for English. Not only are the British incorrigible punners and ardent crossword puzzlers, but many are also enthralled by the history and diversity of the native tongue. And while the British love to complain about its quirky grammar and inconsistent spelling, I wonder how many would really want it otherwise. All this weirdness makes for excellent stories. What more could one wish for?

Well, how about the life of other languages? In both their spoken and written forms, Europe's scores of languages may sound and look forbidding, but the stories about them are compelling. This book sets out to tell sixty of the best. You will hear how French, seemingly so mature, is really guided by a mother fixation. You will discover why Spanish sounds like a submachine gun. And if you thought German spread across Europe at gunpoint, prepare to be proved wrong. You will also venture further afield, as we explore the oddly democratic nature of Norwegian, the gender-bending tendencies of Dutch, the bloody battles fought over Greek and the linguistic orphans of the Balkans. Yet further off the beaten track you will be guided to the ancient heirlooms of Lithuanian, the snobbery of Sorbian and the baffling ways of Basque. And believe it or not, some of Europe's most incredible language stories are to be found right on Britain's doorstep – outlandish and inlandish at the same time, so to speak, in the islands' Celtic and travellers' tongues.

Lingo is a guidebook of sorts, but in no sense an encyclopedia: while some chapters are short portraits of entire languages, others centre on an individual quirk or personality. It is intended, as the French so enticingly put it, as an *amuse-bouche*.

Gaston Dorren, 2014

These two **symbols** are used at the end of each section, mainly to entertain. ⇆ introduces a word or two that English has loaned from the language under discussion, while ⚲ highlights a word that doesn't exist in English – but perhaps should.

PART ONE

Next of tongue

Languages and their families

Europe's two big language families are Indo-European and Finno-Ugric. The lineage of Finno-Ugric is fairly straightforward, as are its modern variants (Finnish, Hungarian, Estonian). But the pedigree of the Indo-Europeans is a real tangle that ranges through Germanic, Romance and Slavic languages, and more. In some respects, though, its story is like any other family saga, complete with conservative patriarchs (Lithuanian), bickering children (Romansh), spitting-image siblings (the Slavics), forgotten cousins (Ossetian), orphans (Romanian and other Balkan languages) and kids who find it hard to cut the apron strings (French).

Nymes

Jngermen

Liflland

Otf

Jeszi. u

Land

Posuet

LITHVANICA

Tewe musu kurse

dangus. Szweski

1

The life of PIE

Lithuanian

Once upon a time, thousands of years ago (nobody knows quite when), in a faraway land (nobody knows quite where), there was a language that no one speaks today and whose name has been forgotten, if it ever had one. Children learned this language from their parents, just as children today do, and they in turn passed it on to their children, and so on and so forth, for generation after generation. In the course of all the centuries, the old language underwent constant change. It was a bit like Chinese whispers: the last player hearing something quite different from what the first actually said. In this case, the last players are us.

And not only those of us who speak English, of course. Those who speak Dutch, too – which is practically the same thing. And German, which is not so different either. And Spanish and Polish and Greek, because if you look closely enough you'll see that even they look a bit like English. Further afield there are other languages, like Armenian and Kurdish and Nepalese, where you have to look quite a bit harder still to see the family resemblance. But each and every one of them emerged from a language that was spoken by a people whose name we don't know, perhaps sixty centuries ago. And because no one knows what their language was called, a name has been invented for it: PIE.

PIE stands for *Proto-Indo-European*. This is not a perfect name. The word *proto* ('first') implies that no language preceded it, which is not the case, while the label 'Indo-European' suggests a language area that's confined to India to Europe. In fact, almost everyone in the Americas speaks a language that's descended from PIE, while in India more than 200 million people speak languages that have no historical ties to PIE at all. That said, more than 95 per cent of Europeans now speak an Indo-European language – in other words, a language evolved from PIE.

PIE and its speakers are shrouded in the mists of time, but linguists are working hard to dispel the fog by reconstructing how PIE may have sounded, on the basis of its descendants. Old documents in ancient languages such as Latin, Greek and Sanskrit are particularly useful for this, but there's a role for more recent sources, too, ranging from Irish ogham inscriptions (fourth century) and the Old English *Beowulf* (ninth century or thereabouts) to the first written remnants of Albanian (fifteenth century) and even modern Lithuanian dialects.

To reconstruct the PIE word for 'tongue', for example, linguists will look at the words that these later languages use, such as *lezu, liežuvis, tengae, tunga, dingua, gjuhë, käntu, językŭ* and *jihva* (taken from Armenian, Lithuanian, Old Irish, Swedish, Old Latin, Albanian, Tocharian A, Old Slavic and Sanskrit, respectively). At first glance these have little in common. But if you compare series like these in a systematic way, all sorts of patterns emerge. It gradually becomes clear that language A has changed ('corrupted', if you like) PIE words consistently in one way, whereas language B has changed them consistently in another. Once you've identified these processes, you can work your way back to the original word.

A MAP OF EUROPEAN LANGUAGES (1741) WITH THE FIRST LINES OF THE
LORD'S PRAYER IN LITHUANIAN.

This kind of detective work has yielded a great deal of
information. Unfortunately, though, the results are not greatly
enlightening for non-linguists. 'Tongue', as it turns out, appears
to have been *$dn\acute{g}^hwéh_2s$ in PIE. The asterisk here signifies that the
word has been reconstructed on the basis of later languages. The
other characters all represent a sound – but as to which sound,
only specialists can tell (and, even for them, some sounds remain
obscure). The result, in short, is rather abstract and not readily
comprehensible.

Is there any way to bridge the divide between the language of
our distant ancestors and ourselves? Can we not make PIE more
accessible, its speakers more human? Can we bring the language
and the people to life? The answer is yes, to some extent. And
Vilnius, the capital of Lithuania, is a good place to do it.

Vilnius is the birthplace of Marija Gimbutas (1921–1994), a
linguist who, in the 1950s, came up with the so-called 'Kurgan

hypothesis', which located the speakers of PIE in the vast steppes north of the Black and Caspian seas (today's Ukraine and southern Russia) around 3700 BC. 'Kurgan' is a Turkic word for a tumulus, and is applied to ancient burial mounds that are found all over this region. Gimbutas proposed that the culture that produced some of these mounds – a culture sufficiently developed to have tamed horses and even ridden chariots – would have been the source of PIE. Though her theory is not entirely uncontroversial, the gist of it has gained wide acceptance.

And if you're keen to get up close and personal with PIE, Vilnius is your best destination, because of all the world's living languages, Lithuanian is the one that most closely resembles PIE. Today's Lithuanians might not be able to chat with the Indo-Europeans of old, but they would be able to get a grip on the language a lot faster than a Greek or Nepali, let alone a Brit. The similarities are many. 'Son', for example, is *sūnus* in Lithuanian and **suh₂nus* in PIE. *Esmi* in PIE means 'I am', as it does in some Lithuanian dialects (though the modern standard language of Vilnius uses *esu* instead). The Lithuanian language has preserved the sounds of many PIE words, while other languages have moved on – in the case of English, in a move so drastic that it's known as the Great Vowel Shift. Consider the word 'five', for example. Both the English word and the Lithuanian *penki* are descendants of **penkʷe*. But only an expert can spot any resemblance between **penkʷe* and the English 'five', while anyone can see the likeness in the Lithuanian word.

Perhaps even more striking are the grammatical similarities. PIE had eight cases, and Lithuanian still has seven. Other languages, such as Polish, also have seven cases, but only in Lithuanian do the cases still sound a lot like those in PIE. Similarly, like PIE, some Lithuanian dialects have not just the regular singular and plural forms, but also a special 'dual': a plural referring specifically to two things. This is rare among modern Indo-European languages, Slovene being the major – and proud – exception.

Verb conjugations, syntax, emphasis patterns, suffixes – many features of Lithuanian testify to its PIE origins. All of them have survived for two hundred generations with relatively little alteration. Lithuanians, therefore, are the undisputed European champions of Chinese whispers.

....

⇆ While PIE stands at the root of English, Lithuanian has handed almost no words to English. The word 'eland', for a South African antelope, may have come from Lithuanian (*élnis*) but only via Dutch and German (where it means 'elk').

....

⚯ *Rudenėja* – the Lithuanian word for the beginning of autumn, as manifested in nature.

2

The separated siblings

Finno-Ugric Languages

What language do Finnish tourists in Hungary speak? 'English' might be your immediate answer, and you would probably be right. Finnish and Hungarian are related (they belong to the Finno-Ugric family, sometimes known as the Uralic), but they are simply too different for Finns to have a hope of making themselves understood in Budapest if they stick to their mother tongue. This linguistic distance reflects not geographic distance, but historical distance. Living far apart needn't be a problem – as Australians and the English prove. Spending a very long time apart, however, is a different proposition.

And the period of separation between the Finns and the Hungarians is a long time indeed: their linguistic ancestors went their separate ways more than 4,000 years ago. At that time, the changes that were to make English different from Russian and Greek and Hindi were yet to take place.

And yet, if you look very closely, there are many similarities between Finnish and Hungarian. For one thing, they have a few hundred so-called *cognates*, literally 'born-together' words, which share the same origin. A famous sentence to illustrate this is 'The living fish swims underwater.' The Finnish translation is *Elävä kala ui veden alla*; in Hungarian it runs *Eleven hal úszkál a víz alatt*. With other cognates, the resemblance can be rather less obvious. Historical linguists are positive, for example, that *viisi* and *öt* ('five') are cognate pairs, as are *juoda* and *iszik* ('drink'), *vuode* and *ágy* ('bed'), and *sula-* and *olvad* ('melt'). But it's not so clear to the rest of us, even to a Finn or Hungarian.

So how can linguists be sure that the connections are there? Well, there are some twenty other languages, most of them small and spoken in northwest Russia, that form a bridge over the abyss that separates Hungarian and Finnish. The word for 'five', for instance, takes on forms such as *viit* (in Estonian), *vit* (Komi), *wet* (Khanty) and *ät* (Mansi), a sequence that neatly joins the Finnish *viisi* to the Hungarian *öt*.

And vocabulary is of course just one aspect of language. When it comes to phonology (the sounds of a language) and grammar, the kinship of Hungarian and Finnish is easier to see. In terms of sounds, both have a large set of vowels, which is exceptional in itself. More tellingly, among these vowels are two that English and most other languages don't have – they are equivalent to *eu* and *u* in French, or *ö* and *ü* in German. What's more, both languages divide their vowels into two sets, and all vowels within each individual word have to belong to the same set. Finally, all words are stressed on the first syllable.

Finnish and Hungarian also share at least six grammatical features that are rare in Europe. Both of them ignore gender to the point where they have only one word for 'he' and 'she' (*hän* in Finnish, *ő* in Hungarian). Both have more than twelve cases. Both have postpositions rather than prepositions. Both have a great love of suffixes – a word along the lines of *establishmentarianistically*, consisting mostly of suffixes, wouldn't raise an eyebrow. Possession is expressed not with a verb but with

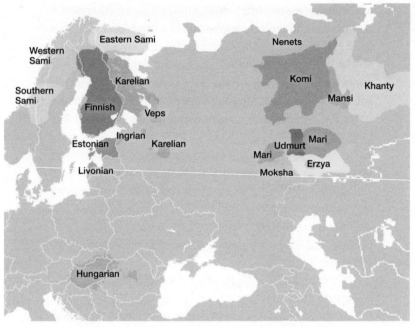

THE FINNO-UGRIC WORLD – A SOMEWHAT LONELY AND DISCONNECTED
PLACE IF YOU STRAY TOO FAR FROM FINLAND AND ESTONIA.

a suffix; instead of saying 'I have it', they say something that could
be rendered in English as 'it is on me'. And finally, numerals are
always followed by a singular ('six dog' rather then 'six dogs'); if
the number has been made explicit, why go to the extra trouble
of modifying what follows?

Surely all these similarities are enough to convince you that
Finnish and Hungarian are siblings? But here's a twist. Nearly all
of the phonological and grammar similarities between these two
are *also* shared by Turkish. So you could think there's another
family member here. And that's exactly what linguists used to
think, and some still do. Most, however, now feel that in spite of
the similarities, the evidence is inconclusive. They prefer to keep
Turkish separate from the other two, arguing that the similarities

22

are explained partly by chance, partly by influence. (Hungarians and speakers of Turkic languages have a history of contact that goes quite far back.)

Yet it *could* be true. We just can't be sure. If only there were languages, however small and endangered, to bridge the gap between Turkish and Hungarian. They may never have existed, or they've become extinct. We'll probably never know.

....

⇆ ☝ For Finno-Ugric loan-words and words that ought to be imported into English, see the individual chapters on Estonian, Finnish, Hungarian and Sami.

3

Pieces of a broken pitcher

Romansh

Romansh. Let's see ... that's the odd little language they speak in Switzerland, isn't it? The fourth national language, alongside French, Italian and a weird form of German? Yes, is the short, boring and mildly inaccurate answer. But for the long answer we need to travel back in time, twenty centuries or so.

Rome is at the height of its power. Like an almighty earthenware pitcher, the Roman Empire contains the entire Mediterranean region, with the Strait of Gibraltar as its mouth. But pottery doesn't last forever: in the fifth century, the empire falls apart. The east, with its predominantly Greek culture, manages to stay intact; though steadily crumbling, it will preserve its unity for many centuries to come. But the western half shatters fully and forever. And with it, Latin, too, splinters into many different pieces. With less and less contact between regions, their speech evolves into separate dialects. Meanwhile, various different tribes, each with their own language, settle all over the former empire. Some of them take up the local Latin, then give it their own flavour.

These shards of Latin eventually developed into the Romance languages: the five big ones – Italian, French, Spanish, Portuguese and the eastern outlier, Romanian – and a plethora of others. But the emergence of the Big Five took a very long time. In the immediately post-Roman centuries, Latin disintegrated not into five, but into dozens of languages, and as many dialects as there are drops of water in a pitcher. Traversing the territories of the former Roman Empire around the year 1200, you would find no two cities that shared the same language. Every last village had its own village Latin.

The rise of what we now call the Romance languages began some time later. Kings such as Denis of Portugal and Alfonso X of Spain, literary greats such as Dante and institutions like the Académie Française helped to glue the shards of local dialects into languages that were used over larger areas, mostly in writing at first. The Big Five were the most successful: they became the official languages of nation states, and even – in the case of Spanish, Portuguese and French – of new empires.

But other groups of Roman dialects also worked their way to full-blown language status. In Spain, two minority Romance languages are now nationally recognised: Catalan on the east coast, and Galician in the northwest corner. Just east of Galician can be found a group of closely related languages – Asturian, Leonese and (in Portugal) the small Mirandese – that play only regional roles. In France, in addition to French (with its many different dialects), Occitan, Corsican and Arpitan are all separate languages, whatever Paris may think. In Italy, where every dialect is the pride of its region, some can also stake a claim to separate language status. Sardinian has the best credentials, but Venetian and a good ten others have reasonably strong cases. Three varieties of Romanian have emerged that may well be considered independent languages: Aromanian, spoken in various southern Balkan countries; Megleno-Romanian, used in Greece

THIS SWISS SIGN ON THE MATTERHORN HAS 'DO NOT CROSS THE RAILWAY LINES', IN FIVE LANGUAGES, ROMANSH FIRST, JAPANESE LAST.

and Macedonia; and Istro-Romanian, spoken on the Croatian peninsula of Istria but now almost extinct. Also native to Istria is Istriot, a Romance language of obscure lineage. Now spoken only by a few hundred older people, it will probably die out before the experts have solved the riddle of its pedigree. Other Romance languages have already expired: Dalmatian, in the late nineteenth century, was the most recent death in the family.

So where does this leave Romansh? Well, the situation is complicated. Romansh is recognised by the Swiss constitution and some 35,000 people in the canton of Graubünden speak the language, but in forms that vary from valley to valley. Even a simple word like 'I' varies from *eu* to *ja*. 'How nice' is *che bel* in one dialect, *tgei bi* in another. The upshot is that Romansh speakers from one village have great difficulty understanding villagers who live just a few kilometres away. Had all these dialects not been so isolated for centuries, they would have been absorbed into bigger languages. Had they had their own city, to act as a cultural centre, they would have combined into a single language. Instead, they remain today what they always have been: splinters of the broken pitcher once called Latin.

So which dialect do Switzerland and Graubünden recognise as 'true' Romansh? Until a generation ago, the answer was: not one of them, but all of them. School books were published in five different variants. It was only in 1982, after a series of failed attempts, that these fragments were glued together into one standard language, *Rumantsch Grischun* (Graubünden Romansh). For reasons of neutrality, the commissioning body, the *Lia Rumantscha* (Romansh League), gave the job to an outsider, the German-speaking linguist Heinrich Schmid. The canton and the central government have embraced Schmid's creation with open arms, and they now publish laws and school books and all sorts of things in the new, unified language. But neutral or not, the standard language has failed to conquer the hearts of the dialect speakers. The majority of Graubünden municipalities still use their own local dialect as their first language.

And Romansh is not the only Romance language that has gone its own regional way. It belongs to a group of three such stubborn outsiders, together called the Rhaeto-Romance sub-family. The other two are spoken in Italy: Ladin and Friulian. Ladin, with its 30,000 speakers bordering the German and Italian language areas, is as hopeless a case as Romansh: every tiny village has a few hundred speakers who fully understand only each other. Friulian, by contrast, is a relatively standardised language. It has more than half a million speakers in the far northeast of Italy, including city dwellers, and a literature that far exceeds the bounds of regional novels and doggerel.

....

⇆ The one and only Romansh word to have entered the English language is 'avalanche', through French.

....

💡 A *giratutona*, literally a 'neck turner', is somebody who trims their sails to every wind. This was voted the most beautiful Romansh word by a jury in 2004.

4

Mummy dearest

French

Modern French has a very strong attachment to its mother. Indeed, something of a mother fixation. You would expect such a seemingly sophisticated language to have long since matured. After all, it's more than a thousand years old, it has cohabited with others, travelled the world. But no – watch French closely and you'll see that it is still clutching at the skirt of its mother: Latin.

It was Julius Caesar who planted the first seeds of French. In the first century BC he and his legions took over Gaul, as France was then known. He came, spoke and conquered, and when the Romans departed five centuries later, the people they left behind spoke Latin. That is to say, soldier's and merchant's Latin, influenced by Gaulish, the Celtic language which the locals had spoken before. The kind of Latin that any serious classicist would be deeply unhappy about. Nevertheless, however adulterated, it was recognisable Latin. Thus was French conceived.

Having ousted Celtic in the preceding five centuries, Latin spent the next five centuries competing against Germanic for dominance in northern Gaul. To be more precise, its opponent was Frankish, the language spoken by the new rulers. Famed medieval kings such as Clovis, Pepin the Short and Charlemagne were all bilingual: while Frankish was their mother tongue, they learnt classical Latin from their tutors. Anyone of any social or intellectual ambition did likewise. Meanwhile the great unwashed continued to speak what was, by now, very bad Latin indeed. So bad, in fact, that it came to be known as *lingua romana rustica*: rustic Roman. Julius Caesar would have turned over in his grave if he had seen what had become of the language he had introduced: of the six Latin cases, only three remained; neuter words had become masculine; and various tenses had changed beyond recognition. In addition to the dozens of Celtic words that had crept in earlier (*charrue*, 'plough'; *mouton*, 'sheep'), many hundreds of Frankish words now came flooding in (*auberge*, 'inn'; *blanc*, 'white'; *choisir*, 'choose').

When an entire people speak a different language from their rulers, eventually one side has to yield. In this case it was the rulers: the tenth-century Frankish king Hugh Capet was the first to speak not Frankish, but the language of his people (alongside the proper Latin he had learnt at school). So the peasant language had finally found its way to the royalty; the *lingua romana rustica* had become *lingua romana* or 'Roman language'. We know it now as Old French, but the designation 'French' (*franceis, françoix, français*) would not come into vogue for several centuries.

Some time later, in Italy, the Renaissance broke out, eventually spreading to all of Western Europe. The whole region came under the spell of classical antiquity, and all Western European languages fell prey to an obsession with the Romans and their language. In this, French outstripped all the others. It wanted to resemble its mother, in as many ways as possible. Words of non-Latin origin – especially Germanic words – fell into disrepute. *Sur* ('sour') was gradually supplanted by the Latin *acide*. *Maint* ('many'), a word tainted with Germanic ancestry, was eclipsed by *beaucoup*.

Long-forgotten words were extracted from classical Latin texts and given new life. *Célèbre*, *génie* and *patriotique* may seem like typically French words, but were in fact imported straight from Latin only at this later stage in the development of the language. The Latin *masticare* ('chew'), which had developed via 'rustic Roman' into *mâcher*, was now revived as *mastiquer*. *Fragilis* ('breakable'), which had been reduced to *frêle*, was reborn as *fragile*. (English, of course, turned them into *masticate*, *frail* and *fragile*.)

THE ROMAN ROLE MODEL AT ITS MOST BLATANT IN THIS IDEALISED SCULPTURE OF NAPOLEON.

To resemble your mother, sounding similar is not enough. You also have to *look* the same – wear her skirts, put on her lipstick, the whole works. The French language is replete with silent consonants that are the heirlooms of its Latin parent. Thousands of *c*'s, *d*'s, *f*'s, *h*'s, *l*'s, *p*'s, *r*'s, *s*'s, *t*'s, *x*'s and *z*'s appear on paper without ever being spoken. For example, *temps* ('time', 'weather') sounds like 'tã' (pronounced through the nose, hence the tilde above the *a*). *Tant* ('so much') sounds exactly the same. But the former comes from the Latin *tempus*, the latter from *tantus* – hence the two spellings. (English has on several occasions done the same. The *b* in *debt*, for instance, was never pronounced, but comes from the Latin word *debere*, meaning 'owe'.) Another example: the word *homme* ('man', 'human being') starts with an *h*, which the French, famously, can't pronounce. This is because the Latin word from which it is derived, *homo,* started with an *h*.

Some of these silent consonants can be heard when the following word starts with a vowel. *Prenez* ('take'), for example, sounds like 'prnay', but *prenez-en* ('take some') sounds more like 'prnay-zã'. Another example: the *s* in the word *les* (plural 'the') is normally silent, but in *les amis* ('the friends') it is pronounced: 'lez-ah-mee'. Again, it's the Latin showing through: *les* is the continuation of the Latin demonstratives *illos/illas* ('those'), and the mostly silent French plurals is the continuation of the (pronounced) final *s* of those Latin words.

The situation changes whenever the French want to sound their Sunday best. Then, suddenly, many more of these usually suppressed consonants can be heard. In *tu as attendu* ('you have waited'), for instance, they start pronouncing the *s* as well. In their workaday speech, they wouldn't dream of doing such a thing – but it just sounds so irresistibly *distinguished*. And probably it sounds distinguished because it's such a hard thing to do: the speaker, while speaking, has to see the words spelt out before they utter them. In other words, the self-respecting

French speaker has to keep the image of mother Latin in mind at all times, because French has been modelled in her image, and dressed up in her spelling.

If that's not an unhealthy mother fixation, what is?

....

⇆ French is second only to Latin as a donor of loanwords to the English language. It has given thousands, ranging from the workaday 'air' and 'place' to the grander *maître d'* and *je ne sais quoi*.

....

💡 *Terroir* – a place where a crop is grown, made unique by its geographic, geologic and climatic characteristics. Used mostly by wine connoisseurs, but applicable to any other produce. It is actually on its way to adoption in English – among foodies, at least.

5

Know your Slovek from your Slovane

Slavic languages

All Slavic languages look a lot like each other. So if you know one of them, you know a whole bunch – it's the linguistic equivalent of a bargain offer.

Take the word for 'Slavic', for example. In Russian it's *slavjanski*, in Polish *słowiański* and in Serbo-Croatian *slavenski*. And these are languages that are fairly far removed from one another, belonging as they do to three different groups: the East, West and South Slavic branches, respectively. Another good example is the word for 'word': *slovo* in Ukrainian, *slovo* in Slovak and *slovo* in Bulgarian – once again, East, West and South.

But, now and then, this resemblance becomes more of a headache than a help. As it turns out, *slovenský* is the Czech word for – no, not 'Slovene', as you might have guessed, but 'Slovak'. The word for 'Slovene', in fact, is *slovinský*. Along with *slovinský* and *slovenský*, Czech also has *slovanský*, 'Slavic'. In Bulgarian, *slovenski* does mean 'Slovene', but in Macedonian it means 'Slavic'.

And *slovinski* in Macedonian refers to Slovincian, an extinct dialect from Poland which, incidentally, the Czechs call ... well, you get the picture.

So if you know one Slavic language, you know a whole bunch of them – the only problem is, often you don't know which one it is that you know. Was it Slovak that calls itself *slovenčina* and Slovene *slovenščina*, or vice versa? Looking it up is no easy task either – is a Slovene–Slovak dictionary a *slovinsko-slovenský slovník* in Slovene and a *slovensko-slovaški slovar* in Slovak, or was it the other way round? And which of these languages was it that – on top of *slovinčina* and *slovenčina* – also has the word *slovienčina*, meaning 'Slavic language'? Not to mention the Slavic languages Serbian and Sorbian, which both happen to be called *Srbský* in Slovene – correction: in Slovak.

It seems like a bargain, all these Slavic languages looking pretty much the same. And for Miroslav, Stanislav and other Slavs, it *is* a dozen for the price of one. But for the rest of us, it's best not to be too greedy.

....

⇆ ☝ For Slavic loan-words and words that ought to be imported into English, see the individual chapters on Slovak, Slovene, Czech, Serbo-Croatian, Sorbian, Polish, Bulgarian, Macedonian, Russian, Belarusian and Ukrainian.

6

The linguistic orphanage

Balkan languages

Your family makes you who you are. You inherit your genes from your parents, who inherited theirs from theirs. Most languages, likewise, are part of a family, and the members of those families share certain inherited characteristics. Of course, in linguistic reproduction, new languages are not born from the conjunction of two parent languages, which rather puts paid to our biological metaphor. Generally, languages divide into separate parts, like amoebas, or develop offshoots, like strawberry plants. For instance, the Romance languages (Romanian, French, Italian and more) evolved from Latin, and Tok Pisin (the creole language of Papua New Guinea) is a young offshoot of English.

But our family lineage is not the only thing that determines how we, as people, behave, dress and express ourselves. Our experiences and the people who cross our paths also make us who we are. As a result, some family members seem to stand out more than others – the proverbial 'white ravens' or, more often than not, the black sheep of the family. This pattern certainly applies to matters linguistic. Languages can have a strong influence on one another, particularly in areas where different language families live in close contact for centuries. And nowhere else in Europe has this happened more intensively and intricately – and with more lasting effect – than in the Balkans.

Forming the southeast corner of the European continent, the Balkans is home to a jumble of languages – from Albanian, Bulgarian, Greek and Macedonian to Romanian, Romani, Serbo-Croatian and Turkish – which no longer live with their families, so to speak. In fact, Albanian and Greek have no family left. Romanian lives hundreds of kilometres from its nearest Romance relative, Italian. Romani, an Indian language, is thousands of kilometres from its family in South Asia, while most of the siblings of Turkish are quite some way to the east. Finally, the Slavic Balkan languages (Bulgarian, Macedonian and Serbo-Croatian) form a contiguous group with Slovenian, but they, too, have all been isolated from the bulk of their relatives (such as Russian, Ukrainian and Polish). In short, the Balkans is something of a linguistic orphanage.

Turkish is a bit of an introvert. In its contact with the other languages, it has done little more than borrow and, in particular, lend words. The other seven, by contrast, have influenced one another profoundly – no surprise given that they've long shared the same premises. For centuries the speakers of these languages have married, migrated, lived, travelled and traded together, been to war as both enemies and allies, and interfered in each other's religions. Even now, in the twenty-first century, the Balkans are teeming with minorities. There are Serbian-speaking enclaves in Albanian-speaking areas, Macedonian and Romanian enclaves in Greek areas, and so on and so forth. In the past, the population was even more of a hotch-potch than it is today, with just about everyone knowing two or more languages – not necessarily fluently, but well enough to communicate.

As a result of all this multilingualism, languages that were once as different as night and day slowly started resembling one another, most particularly Romanian, Albanian, Macedonian and Bulgarian. Nowadays, they share so many similarities they could all be mistaken for kin (Macedonian and Bulgarian are indeed closely related, but the other two are not). Serbo-Croatian, Greek and Romani have also come to share several traits with this linguistic quartet. Together, this ensemble forms the so-called Balkan *sprachbund* – a kind of Balkan League.

So what do they have in common? Articles, for one thing. Unlike us, most League members attach the definite article ('the') to the end of the noun instead of putting it in front. In Romanian, for example, 'dog' is *câine* and 'the dog' is *câinele*. In Bulgarian these would be *kuche* and *kucheto*, where the extra letters at the end signify the article, and in Albanian *qen* and *qeni*. This is noteworthy, differing as it does from the behaviour of the closest relatives of these languages (Italian and Polish, for example). As the linguists Joachim Matzinger and Stefan Schumacher (see p.235) discovered some years ago, the source of this particular custom is probably Albanian.

Another typical Balkan feature is the tendency to make sparing use of the infinitive, or to avoid it altogether. In most European languages, infinitives are widely used in sentences like 'he ought to go'. Romanian and most other Balkan languages, however, prefer to use conjugated verb forms, resulting in sentences that would translate literally as 'it ought that he goes'. This trait, too, is not seen in related languages outside the Balkans.

A third noteworthy feature is the formation of the future tense, recognisable in English by the word 'will'. European languages have different ways of expressing this tense, but the Balkan League members are (almost) unique in doing so by the use of a single, invariant word. The original meaning of this

THEIR LANGUAGE HAS BEEN INFLUENCED STRONGLY BY ITS BALKAN
NEIGHBOURS, BUT ROMANIANS ARE PROUD OF ITS LATIN ROOTS.

word was something like '(it) wants', but it has since become
purely a grammatical tool. As an example, 'they will sing' is *ei
vor cânte* in Romanian, which once meant '(it) wants that they
sing'. (Incidentally, English could easily be a Balkan language in
this regard, as 'they will' was once synonymous with 'they want'
or 'they wish'.)

And the similarities continue. Most Balkan League members
do not form degrees of comparison with suffixes ('prettier',

'prettiest', etc.) but with auxiliary words ('more pretty', 'most pretty'). Several members have only two or three grammatical cases, one of which is invariably the vocative. And various members also have a dull 'uh' sound, known as a schwa, which is the sound of the English 'a' in *sofa*, or the 'i' in pencil or the 'e' in *spoken*. The Romanian *ă*, the Albanian *ë* and the (Cyrillic) *ъ* in Bulgarian are all pronounced like this.

All this might seem like good news. The more similarities these languages share, the better their people can communicate. Or so you might think. But the Balkan languages differ in one crucial respect: their vocabulary. Of course, they share certain similarities. It's no coincidence that the word for 'dog' is similar in Romanian (*câine*) and Albanian (*qen*), given that both are derived from the Latin *canis*. The word for 'paint' likewise shares a common origin: the Albanian *bojë*, the Romanian *boia*, the Romani *bojava* and the Bulgarian, Macedonian and Serbo-Croatian *boja* all stem from the Turkish *boya*. But, with the exception of the three Slavic languages, the differences in vocabulary greatly outweigh the similarities.

So throughout their centuries in the orphanage, the grammatical behaviour of the various Balkan languages grew closer. But in terms of outer appearance – their vocabulary – they remained stubbornly loyal to their families. The result: despite the similarities, their speakers can't understand one another.

....

⇆ English borrowed 'pastrami' from Yiddish, which had it from Romanian, which had in turn borrowed it from Greek or Turkish. The name Dracula is Romanian for 'devil'.

....

💡 *Omenie* – a Romanian word for the virtue of being fully human, that is: gentle, decent, respectful, hospitable, honest, polite.

7

The tenth branch

Ossetian

The former Soviet Union is teeming with languages. Tabasarran, Talysh, Tatar, Tsakhur, Tsez, Tindi and Ter Sami – those are just the Ts that you'll find in the European part of Russia. Kabardian, Kalmyk, Karachay-Balkar, Karata, Karelian, Khwarshi, Kildin Sami and Komi – those are the Ks in the same region. Many dozens of minorities live in the territories of the former USSR, and they all have their own tongues. A book covering the whole lot would be immense, and interesting only to specialists. This chapter is going to take a look at just one of these obscure languages: Ossetian. It's spoken by a few hundred thousand people in an area straddling the border between Russia and Georgia, but there is something about Ossetian that makes it very noteworthy.

First, though, a little preamble. Almost all the languages of Europe belong, as noted, to the Indo-European family. This is the world's largest language family, with hundreds of members and around three billion speakers. The languages are spread across ten branches: five large and five small. The three smallest branches are Albanian, Armenian and Greek, which each represent exactly one

THE ENDANGERED SNOW LEOPARD, FRONTING THE SEVEN MOUNTAINS OF
OSSETIA, ON SOUTH OSSETIA'S COAT OF ARMS.

living standard language. The Baltic branch has two 'leaves', Latvian
and Lithuanian. The Celtic branch has four living languages (and
two undead: Cornish and Manx), but between them they have fewer
than a million native speakers, making this branch more of a small,
withered twig. Then there are the five big branches. Three of these
will sound familiar: Germanic, Romance and Slavic. These groups
include, respectively, English, French and Russian.

We've now accounted for the eight European branches of the
Indo-European family. Some of these languages are also spoken
elsewhere, though their home is clearly in Europe or, in the case of
Armenian, just a stone's throw away. But the name Indo-European
suggests that there is also an Indian branch. And indeed there
is – branch number nine encompasses languages such as Hindi
and Bengali. The tenth branch, finally, is made up of the Iranian
languages found in the broad strip of land between the Indian region
and Europe, running from eastern Turkey (Kurdish) to Tajikistan
(Tajik, a form of Persian).

So there is a clear dichotomy: there are eight branches of the Indo-European family in Europe, and two in Asia. But the best bit of every rule is the exception – and in this case there are two. The first is Romani, the Indic language of the Roma (some of them, anyway), who originally came from India. The other exception is – you guessed it, Ossetian. And this is what makes Ossetian so interesting: it's the language that ensures that the Iranian group, too, is represented in Europe. In other words, all ten of the Indo-European branches can in fact be found *within* Europe.

⇆ The yoghurt-like drink called *kefir*, borrowed from Russian, is originally a word from a Causasus language, with Ossetian *k'æpý* one of the candidates.

💡 *Kærts* condenses 'sheepskin coat' into a single word.

PART TWO

Past perfect discontinuous

Languages and their history

Some languages are small, while others are spoken by millions of people across vast areas. But the giants had humble beginnings (German, Galician), and some of the smaller ones had a more glorious past (Danish, Norman, the Jewish languages). And in the case of Icelandic, the past and present are much the same thing.

ini z p̄ hir. bi. hc̄ legrat giaina
ā m noꝛuni narī um hnar hc
bellat p er hꝛob ꜹ at g̃t. alp

ioꝰ huaine h̄ uar bear mbill

8

The peaceful expansionist?

German

Most of the major languages of the world have a violent, militaristic record. Latin, for example, travelled with the Roman legions as they imposed the Pax Romana on Western Europe. Arabic, likewise, hitched a ride on the back of Islam when it civilised the infidels. English, of course, was the language of the British Empire. Spanish, Russian and Turkish, too, all emerged bigger and stronger from bloodbaths perpetrated by their speakers. And with size came greater cultural influence.

The story is – perhaps surprisingly – rather different when it comes to the most widely spoken native language in the European Union: German. The German-speaking world has of course not always been devoted to the cause of peace. But little of the growth of the language area, and of the language's sphere of influence, can be attributed to forceful occupation. Quite the opposite, in fact: violence led to the reversal of most of its earlier gains.

Going back to the year 1000, we find the German dialects already covering a sizeable chunk of Central Europe. On the map this territory looks fairly familiar, corresponding roughly with today's German language area, minus the easternmost part. But three growth spurts then brought about considerable expansion.

The first of these lasted from the twelfth to the fourteenth century, and it took various forms. During this period, farmers all over Europe were bringing more and more land under cultivation. The areas to the east of the German lands were very sparsely populated, and German farmers made their way there in large numbers, often at the invitation of the local rulers. Tracts of present-day Poland, Czech Republic and eastern Germany thus became fully Germanised. In other parts of present-day Slovakia, Hungary, Romania and Slovenia, German enclaves also emerged in the midst of the indigenous populations. They were rarely seen as aliens. The region was already a mishmash of languages and ethnic groups, and only much later – with the rise of the 'one people, one nation' orthodoxy – did this ethnic fragmentation in Eastern Europe become a problem.

In the thirteenth and fourteenth centuries, furthermore, large numbers of German Jews fled anti-Semitic pogroms in their homelands in central and southern Germany, mainly heading east towards present-day Poland, Lithuania and Belarus. While the language they took with them, Yiddish, was not exactly German, it had its roots in various German dialects. (Even today, Germans can understand Yiddish if it's written in the Latin alphabet.) Also in the fourteenth century, the Hanseatic League, which was headquartered in the northern port city of Lübeck, was achieving domination of Baltic and North Sea commerce, a position it maintained for a considerable time. The Scandinavians didn't give up their own languages, it's true, but the impact of the Hanseatic traders was immense – between a quarter and one third of modern Danish, Swedish and Norwegian vocabulary is derived from the Low German spoken in northern Germany at the time.

And then there was yet another form of expansion: in the thirteenth century, the Teutonic Knights, a militaristic religious

46

TEUTONIC ORDER CASTLE IN PAIDE, ESTONIA.

order that grew out of the Crusades, conquered and converted the region that now comprises Estonia and Latvia. For many centuries, a German-speaking elite would rule the roost here. This is perhaps the only example of a long-term expansion of the German language being achieved by military means.

All things considered, then, German had enormous presence and influence in Central, Northern and Eastern Europe around 1400. For quite some time, that's where it stayed. The German populations, devastated by the Black Death in the middle of the fourteenth century, had all the land they needed. The Hanseatic League fell into a slow decline, and from 1618 to 1648 the German lands were ravaged by the Thirty Years War. And yet, not long after the conflict, a second growth spurt began. Again, German farmers made for present-day Poland, followed by large numbers heading into Russia on the invitation of rulers such as Catherine the Great, to cultivate land that was either empty or inhabited by non-Russian tribes. And Germany's cultural influence was growing all the time. With the Enlightenment and the Romantic movement, German literature and philosophy spread to all corners of the Western world, and in the nineteenth century Germany became a global powerhouse of science, technology and scholarship. Professors in all subjects, in Europe and in America, found it necessary to read German, which for a few years in the early twentieth century overtook English and French as the primary language of scholarly publication.

In the late nineteenth century, Germany also acquired a number of colonies in Africa and the Pacific, including Namibia and the Solomon Islands – and here, of course, the expansion of the German language was anything but peaceable. Indeed, the atrocities committed by the Germans in Africa were as appalling as anything perpetrated by any European colonial power. And when Germany lost the First World War, it was forced to cede its overseas territories (as well as some border areas in the east and west of Germany itself) to the victors. Except in Namibia, where some 30,000 people have German as a mother tongue, the short-lived colonial administrations left few linguistic traces. Insofar as Germany is still spoken outside Europe, such as in South and North America, this is a result mainly of emigration rather than colonisation.

Despite the loss of the colonies, in the early 1930s the German language was enjoying a stronger position than ever before, and was spoken across a large part of Europe. Fifteen years later, however, everything changed. Whereas the First World War nibbled at the German language area, the aftermath of the Second World War took great chunks out of it. By the end of the 1940s virtually all German speakers had been driven out of Poland, Czechoslovakia and the Baltic states – an exodus of millions. Many German speakers also left the other Eastern European countries, voluntarily or otherwise, and those who remained behind became assimilated into their local culture. The mass murder of the Jews by the Germans meant that Yiddish, the sister language, was largely wiped out; the survivors have, for the most part, left Europe and not transferred the language to their children. A great number of top German scholars moved or were removed to America or the Soviet Union. And English became the ever more dominant language of science.

Centuries of migration, trade and cultural activity had made German a far-flung and highly influential language. The First World War was damaging to the prestige of all things German, but the megalomania and outrageous brutality of the Third Reich had a much greater impact. The German language, you could say, was a victim of the war instigated by its own speakers.

⇆ There are thousands of German loanwords in English. Somewhat unexpected ones include 'noodle', 'abseil', 'seminar' and 'rucksack'. More obvious ones are 'blitz', 'glitz', 'quartz' and 'pretzel'.

💡 *Gönnen* (also spelt as *goennen)* – the exact opposite of 'to envy': to be gladdened by someone else's fortune. Old English had it as *geunnan*, but it seems that English speakers lost the habit.

9

Portugal's mother's tongue

Galician

Welcome to the place where most of this book was written: my study. Were it not for the window blinds, I wouldn't have honoured it with a photo. But it happens that they perfectly illustrate the linguistic history of the Iberian peninsula, especially that of the northwestern tip: Galicia, the region best known for Santiago de Compostela or, if football interests you more than churches or religion, Deportivo de La Coruña.

Galician is very similar to Portuguese. So much so that, were Galicia part of Portugal, the two languages would share one name. As it is, they have different official spellings, and Galician is becoming more like Spanish now that all Galicians know Spanish. But the resemblance is still extremely strong. Galicians and Portuguese can converse with each other without major difficulties. The number of speakers of Galician, three million, is not bad for a regional language, but it's a small club compared to more than two hundred million for Portuguese (ten million in Portugal, the rest in Brazil and Africa). So your inclination might be to see Galician as a sort of child of

THE LINGUISTIC HISTORY OF THE IBERIAN PENINSULA, AS DEPICTED BY
THE BLINDS IN THE AUTHOR'S STUDY.

Portuguese. The truth is, though, that Galician is not the child
– it's the mother.

To explain, we have to go back to the Romans. Between
220 and 19 BC, they conquered the entire Iberian peninsula
and named it Hispania. Latin gradually supplanted the older
languages, except for Basque. Now fast forward to 711 AD. In
that year, Hispania was invaded by the Moors, whose armies
were made up of many North African Berbers and some Arabs,
all of them Muslim. Within a few years they controlled almost
the whole peninsula, from its southern tip to the mountains
in the north. Hispania came to be called Al-Andalus. But while
Arabic became the new official language, Latin remained the
vernacular of most of the inhabitants. At least, that's what they
called it. In fact, the Latin spoken here was so little like Latin that
it really needed a new name. Much later, scholars decided to call
it 'Mozarabic', which is a misleading name, because most people

tend to place the emphasis on the 'Arabic' component, whereas Mozarabic was not a form of Arabic – it was a Romance language with Arabic influences.

Not all of the Iberian peninsula was occupied by the Moors. In the northeast, the Frankish emperor Charlemagne and his successors held a strip just south of the Pyrenees. More importantly, in a mountainous outpost on the north coast, one small Christian kingdom remained: Asturias. This became a hotbed of resistance that fomented the Reconquista, the recapturing of Al-Andalus by the Christian rulers. It was a slow process: around the year 900, only an east-to-west corridor in the north, less than a quarter of all of Hispania, was in Christian hands. This narrow corridor then split into a whole series of small principalities, each with its own Romance language.

And thus we come at last to the windows of my room. In the early tenth century, the situation in the Spanish peninsula looked a lot like what you see here. The right-hand blind can be taken to represent Catalonia, which had made itself independent from the Franks; here, Catalan was spoken. The blind on the left is Galicia, independent now from Asturias, with Galician. And the central blind represents a large area that was divided into several separate kingdoms, including Asturias and Castile. The latter formed the cradle of Spanish, also known as Castilian. The other central kingdoms were home to languages that are today considered to be dialects of Castilian, plus Basque. The visible part of the windows is Al-Andalus, with its Arabic writing and Mozarabic vernacular.

The Christian reconquest of Al-Andalus was completed in 1492. With Hispania now back in the hands of Christian rulers, Mozarabic died out, but the succeeding languages soaked up the many Arabic words it left behind. The entire eastern region of the peninsula now spoke Catalan. The broad chunk in the middle was Spanish speaking, with the stubborn exception of the Basque country. And the whole western strip spoke Galician. In the northern quarter of this strip, Galician was still called Galician (*galego*). But the southern three-quarters of this western strip had by now become a separate country, Portugal, and the Galician spoken here had been renamed 'Portuguese' (*português*). As Portugal became a great maritime nation, it spread its language over all the continents then known to humankind: America (Brazil), Africa (Angola, Mozambique and elsewhere) and Asia (Macau, East Timor).

So Galician went far in the world, but under a Portuguese alias.

....

⇆ The Spanish word *costa*, now integrated into English, seems to be of Galician origin – though it could be Catalan.

....

💡 *Curman* and *curmá* – male and female cousin, respectively. Many languages make this distinction, unlike English.

10

A language in DK

Danish

Two centuries ago, Danish was spoken on four continents in an area twelve times the size of Great Britain. Now, the language is contained in scarcely more than a single country that's just over half the size of Scotland. Read on for a chronicle of ruin.

The decline began in 1814 when Denmark, a loser in the Napoleonic Wars, was forced to cede part of its territory. All of Norway – many times larger than Denmark proper – suddenly gained independence, albeit initially under the rule of the Swedish king. Danish, having been the official language for centuries, had exerted a strong influence on Norwegian, particularly the kind spoken by the urban elite. Norwegian nationalists now had two objectives: out with the Swedish king, and out with the Danish language. It took a while, but eventually they managed both.

The Danish language was also losing ground further afield. In 1839, school students in the Danish West Indies (yes, they existed) were no longer taught in Danish, but in English instead. In 1845, the Danes sold their Indian trading posts to the United Kingdom, and followed suit in 1850 with their West African colonies. And in 1917 the Danish West Indies were sold off as well, this time to the United States. With that, Denmark was no longer a tropical country. Granted, few people actually spoke Danish in these colonies. But in 1864 the motherland itself also took a hit: in the spoils of war, the region of Slesvig was given to Prussia and renamed Schleswig. To this day, the German province of Schleswig-Holstein is home to a Danish-speaking minority numbering tens of thousands.

Then, in 1918, Danish morale took another blow: after more than five centuries under Danish rule, Iceland gained independence. Admittedly, Danish had never been more than an administrative language, but even this status was now lost. Some time later, Iceland also demoted Danish from its position as the most important foreign language. From then on, young Icelanders would focus on English at school instead.

DURING THE LIFETIME OF HANS CHRISTIAN ANDERSEN (1805–1875) DENMARK BEGAN ITS DECLINE, ENDING UP AS AN UGLY DUCKLING.

The Faroe Islands, to the north of Scotland, acquired autonomy within the Danish kingdom in 1948 and promptly declared their native Faroese to be the national language. To help soften the blow, Danish retained its administrative status, but in practice it was used only for official contact with the motherland.

And so all that remained of Denmark's colonies was the largest and most sparsely populated of them all: Greenland. Until 1979, that is, when the island was granted limited autonomy and permission to govern in its own language, Kalaallisut, otherwise known as Greenlandic. This decision came as no great surprise. Although Danish was a mandatory school subject, many Greenlanders struggled to speak the language, which was poles apart from their own. In autonomous Greenland, Danish initially retained more official functions than in the autonomous Faroe Islands. But that has since changed as well: in 2009, Kalaallisut became the one and only official administrative language. With this move, Greenland achieved a unique position: the only country of the Americas (yes, Greenland is part of the Americas), from Canada all the way down to Chile, where the indigenous language doesn't play second fiddle to that of its colonial master.

The poor Danes. Rejected by the Norwegians, betrayed in the warm-water colonies, defeated in Slesvig, then dumped by the cold-water colonies as well. But the Danes do have one consolation: their ancestors were among those who occupied England in the fifth century and thus laid the foundations for English – a language that has conquered the world like no other.

⇆ 'Narwhal' comes from Danish. And 'ugly duckling' is a calque (loan translation) of Hans Christian Andersen's *Den grimme ælling*.

💡 *Farmor* – paternal grandmother. *Morfar*, *farfar* and *mormor* are also available, for the other grandparents.

11

The spoils of defeat

Channel Island Norman

Britain has been conquered many times over. Napoleon and Hitler failed, it's true, but before them was a long line of invaders who came to dominate large parts of the island both politically and culturally. And while their political power waned after a time, their cultural staying power proved to be impressive: Britain owes its linguistic diversity largely to having lost so many battles.

The only non-starter among the conquerors' languages was Dutch, spoken by William of Orange, who took the crown of England, Scotland and Ireland in 1688. The fact that he was invited to invade, by a group of politicians later dubbed the 'Immortal Seven', might have had something to do with it. Even so, he could at least have made an effort to teach Dutch to the British. Instead he switched to English as soon as he set foot on land.

If William comes last in the ranking of linguistically successful invaders of Britain, the frontrunners must be the western Germanic tribes that also came from across the southern North Sea, over a thousand years earlier. Without them – the Angles, the Saxons and probably a sprinkling of Jutes, Frisians and maybe even Franks – there simply would be no English language today. Not in Britain, at any rate. Much of the basic everyday English vocabulary is Anglo-Saxon in origin – *the, a, is, was, in, out, house, town,* et cetera.

These were not the last Germanic tribes to come to the island. From the eighth century onward, Norsemen from Scandinavia raided most of Britain and then began to settle in eastern England and northern Scotland. In England they assimilated fairly soon, though leaving a clear impact on the language – such basic words as *they* and *take* are part of their legacy. In the far north however, especially in Orkney and Shetland, their Norse (or North Germanic or Old Norwegian) developed into a regional language of its own, known as Norn. When the islands became part of the Kingdom of Scotland in the late Middle Ages, Norn began a long and slow decline. So slow, in fact, that the last native speaker died as late as the mid-nineteenth century. So for a thousand years, Britain was home to a North Germanic as well as a West Germanic language. Even today, North Germanic is spoken just 160 miles off the Shetland coast, in the Faroe Islands.

So much for the Germans – or rather, the Germanic people. Let's move on to the Britons. And when I say Britons, I mean the real Celtic Britons, the cultural ancestors of the Welsh. They came from what is now France around 500 BC, or possibly much earlier – their ETA is oddly uncertain. What we do know for sure is that most of them never left, though some of their descendants seem to have fled to Brittany when the Anglo-Saxons arrived, thereby giving this region of France its current name (it was previously called Armorica). In spite of having to share Britain with the expansive and imperialist Anglo-Saxons, the Welsh have managed to maintain their language, although in numbers that dwindled during much of the nineteenth and twentieth centuries. At two and half thousand years or more, they are the undisputed British record-holders for linguistic longevity. Or at least in historic times they are. In what language their predecessors communicated, and for how long, is anybody's guess.

Another Celtic people, the Gaelic-speaking Scots, are unique in that they conquered part of Britain not from the continent but from Ireland. They probably did so in the fourth century AD at the expense of the Picts, whose ethnic and linguistic affiliation is much disputed. Just as Norn survived longest on a couple of islands, Scottish Gaelic has its sturdiest stronghold on the Outer Hebrides.

Anglo-Saxons, Norsemen, two brands of Celts – that makes four waves of invaders, or five if you count William of Orange. And there are two more to be accounted for. Or linguistically speaking just one more, because the two conquerors in question could be said to have brought different versions of the same language – the vintage variety and a remix, so to speak.

The first wave came, of course, with Julius Caesar and his troops, who invaded Britain in 55 BC and then, having completed the conquest of England and Wales, set about building the mod cons of the day: villas, baths, roads and a good strong wall against the Scots. They stayed for four centuries and a half and then left for good. Except that in 1066 the army of William the Bastard arrived, and most of his troops spoke an evolved version of Latin, namely Norman. Norman is markedly different from Latin, but there was never a particular moment in history when people in Normandy stopped speaking Latin and started speaking Norman. One just slowly morphed into the other.

Long before 1066, however, Norman had been influenced by some of the Germanic groups we've already come across: the Franks and the Norsemen. Around the time when a few Franks seem to have joined the Angles, the Saxons and the rest in their one-way trip to Britain, a good deal more of them moved to northern France (ultimately giving the country its current name: it was earlier called Gaul). And around the time when

'LE COUMITÉ DE LA CULTURE GUERNÉSIAISE' HAS A MOTTO: P'TIT, TÊTU,
MAIS PLLOIN D'FORCHE: 'SMALL, STUBBORN, BUT FULL OF STRENGTH'.

some Norsemen were settling in Britain, others found their way
further south and forcefully acquired real estate in Normandy
(giving this region its current name, which was good, because it
doesn't seem to have had one until then). So what William the
Bastard brought to Britain was a late form of Latin, laced with
various Germanic bits.

But as we all know, it wasn't to last. Even though William the
Bastard was crowned king of England and went down in history
as the Conqueror, his Norman language would only ever be the
language of the upper crust. And after a century or two, that crust
crumbled and the ruling classes returned to what had remained
the language of the commoners, English.

Not everywhere, though. To this very day, there is a tiny
minority among the population of the British Islands* that

---

* Under the Interpretation Act of 1978, the term 'British Islands' (as opposed to
  'British Isles', a geographical term in which it is less logical to include the Channel
  Islands) refers to the United Kingdom of Great Britain and Northern Ireland,
  together with Jersey, Guernsey and the Isle of Man. On passports issued to
  residents of the three islands, no mention is made of 'United Kingdom'. Instead,
  the words on the front read 'British Islands' followed by the island's name.

continues to speak Norman. There are nearly six thousand of them and they live on even smaller islands – the Channel Islands. Most of them speak Jèrriais (the Jersey dialect), well over a thousand are fluent in Guernésiais (Guernsey) while perhaps a dozen souls keep Sercquiais alive (Sark). The three varieties are often lumped together as Channel Island Norman, a language that is similar to the Norman spoken on the mainland, as you'd expect, though it's been influenced somewhat by English. Local language lovers are doing their best to save Channel Island Norman from its extinction, but their efforts are nowhere near as spirited as those made in the Isle of Man or even Cornwall. Perhaps, after more than two thousand years, it's time for Latin to leave the British Islands.

⇆ After 1066, English borrowed words from Norman French in a massive way, from 'hostel' to 'very' and from 'castle' to 'warrant'.

💡 *Pap'sée* defines something wrapped up in paper, e.g. *eune pap'sée d'chucrîns* – a quantity of sweets wrapped up in paper. *Ûssel'lie* – the continual opening and closing of doors – is another nice concept.

12

Languages of exile

Karaim, Ladino and Yiddish

For many centuries, from late Classical times to the early Middle Ages, European Jews spoke the languages of the Christian or Muslim majorities among whom they lived. This isn't to say that Jews spoke those languages in exactly the same form as the Gentiles did. For one thing, obviously, the Christian and Muslim majorities lacked the specialised words to describe the concepts and paraphernalia of Jewish faith and cultural tradition. Whatever their language, Jews borrowed these terms from Hebrew and Aramaic, the languages of the Torah and Talmud. Differences between Jewish and non-Jewish speech were also generated by the relative isolation of Jewish communities in places where anti-Semitic sentiment was prevalent. As a result, Jews in many European regions developed their own linguistic varieties, such as Judaeo-Italian, Judaeo-Catalan, Shuadit (Judaeo-Provençal) or Yevanic (Judaeo-Greek).

Many of these Jewish vernaculars were to disappear in later centuries, as a result of emigration, assimilation or genocide. But three of them have a more substantial linguistic place, though emigration, assimilation and persecution were part of their histories as well. The three languages in question are Karaim, Ladino and Yiddish.

The history of Karaim can be traced back to the 1390s, when grand duke Vytautas of Lithuania, a major power at the time, resettled a group of 300 to 400 Jewish families from the newly conquered Crimea within Lithuania proper. These families were part of an ethnic group called the Karaim, whose language belonged to the Turkic family and was closely related to Crimean Tatar. Their resettlement cut them off from their fellow Karaim speakers, but instead of fully assimilating into the local Jewish population, the Karaim maintained their own – and very different – language for hundreds of years. As recently as the early twentieth century it was still very much alive, and even after the horrors of the Holocaust and Stalinism the language retains a small stronghold in the Lithuanian town of Trakai, where several dozen speakers still use it. It's also reported that Karaim is spoken by a tiny number of people in the Crimea and Galicia, in northwest Ukraine.

The story of Ladino begins a century after the Karaim resettlement, on the other side of Europe. In 1492, the so-called Catholic Monarchs of Spain, Queen Isabella I and King Ferdinand II, expelled from Spain all the Jews who wouldn't convert to Christianity. Spain was not unique in taking such a step: King Edward I had banished all 2,000 English Jews two centuries before, after executing several hundred, and some 100,000 Jews had been driven from France in 1396. The difference was in numbers: historians estimate that about a quarter of a million Jews left Spain, resettling throughout the Mediterranean. Particularly large numbers fled to the Ottoman Empire, the continent's rising superpower, which welcomed them wholeheartedly. Indeed, the treatment of Jews under Muslim rulers, while discriminatory, was on the whole much more equitable than in Christian polities.

The language that the Spanish Jews brought with them was at first remarkably close to Christian Spanish, but in the following centuries the two varieties would develop rather differently. Ladino, as Judaeo-Spanish is often called, has retained several fifteenth-century traits that modern Spanish has lost: it distinguishes the 'b' from the 'v' sound, for example, and uses *so* and *sos* for 'I am' and 'you are' instead of *soy* and *eres*. On the other hand, Judaeo-Spanish itself was influenced by its new linguistic neighbours, such as Turkish and Serbo-Croatian, especially in terms of vocabulary. But remarkably, more than five centuries on, Spaniards can still understand Judaeo-Spanish with relative ease. Not that they are likely to hear Ladino on the streets of Madrid, as most of its speakers live in Istanbul or Israel.

The third group of Jews with a markedly different language grew from unremarkable beginnings in the Middle Ages to become the largest Jewish population anywhere in the world, ever. They called themselves Ashkenazim, and their language was Yiddish – from the German word *Jüdisch* for 'Jewish'. Yiddish emerged some time before 1250 (a more precise dating is impossible) among Jews who seem to have come into the German lands from northern France and Italy. They adopted German, while retaining a small number of Romance words and adding the usual Hebrew and Aramaic elements. In the centuries that followed, the core area of the Ashkenazi Jews would shift from Germany, where persecution was intense, to Poland, then a rare haven of religious tolerance in the Christian world. (Smaller numbers would migrate to another such haven, the Dutch Republic.) This core area expanded to include a large swathe of Eastern Europe, including Lithuania, Belarus and parts of Ukraine and Russia.

As a result, Yiddish – like Karaim and Ladino – was now spoken amid majority languages that were very different from the language from which it had arisen, and so it diverged away

IN THE EARLY TWENTIETH CENTURY, YIDDISH WAS SPOKEN BY SOME TEN MILLION JEWS IN MANY COUNTRIES OF EUROPE AND ELSEWHERE. THIS PHOTOGRAPH WAS TAKEN IN NEW YORK IN 1910.

from the old parent. Several sounds were systematically changed, some intricacies of German grammar simplified and numerous words adopted from Polish and other Slavic tongues. Yiddish thrived, and in several areas the number of Yiddish speakers became so large that the Gentile majority languages borrowed a substantial number of (mostly slang) terms from it, as would American English later on. The American English *chutzpah*, for instance, was preceded by the German *Chuzpe*, the Polish *hucpa*, the Czech *chucpe* and the Dutch *gotspe*, among others.

Nowadays European Jews once again speak the languages of the non-Jewish majorities among whom they live, and Karaim, Ladino and Yiddish are all endangered. The Nazi genocide is of course the primary reason for this decline, but it's not the entire explanation. In Germany and the Netherlands, Yiddish fell into disuse in the nineteenth century, as a result of assimilation. Soviet Communism, after initial support for Yiddish and other minority languages, began to Russify all ethnic groups from the 1930s. In

Israel, a revitalised Hebrew was chosen in preference to Yiddish as the national language. And Jews who escaped the Third Reich by fleeing to the USA and elsewhere became assimilated within a generation.

While speakers of Karaim are counted in the tens and those of Ladino in the tens of thousands, Yiddish speakers are estimated at between 1.5 and 3 million worldwide, mostly in the USA and Israel. This may sound an impressive number, but communities where Yiddish is the language of everyday life and where parents transfer it to their children as a matter of course are very rare. (In Europe, the largest communities are in London and Antwerp.) Most people who speak it nowadays are either elderly or have it as a second language. And once those elderly native speakers have died, the future of the language will depend on whether people will still be inclined to learn it.

⇆ While Ladino and Karaim are unrepresented in English, loans from Yiddish are common in slang, including 'tush', 'schmooze', 'klutz' and many more. Exceptionally, there is even a Yiddish loan prefix, *shm*, as in 'politics, shmolitics'.

💡 The best Yiddish words are already absorbed into (American) English.

13

Frozen in time

Icelandic

If you're one of those people who worry that the English language is going to the dogs, linguists are of no help to you. Whatever it is that annoys you – double negatives, the demise of *whom*, the non-standard usage of *literally* – linguists will answer that a language is a living thing, and is always changing. You can't stop the process, so you'd better get used to it.

Examples are plentiful. French, German, Swedish, Hungarian, Basque – the grammar, pronunciation and vocabulary of any language you might name has changed considerably over the centuries, and few more so than English, which has undergone nothing short of an extreme makeover since Anglo-Saxon days. However, there is at least one counter-example: Icelandic. Icelandic is the exception that kills the rule. What is it about this chilly land of hot geysers and volcanoes that makes its language different from the rest?

Its history goes back to the ninth century, when the island was settled by speakers of Old Norse (and probably a sprinkling of Celts, but they soon blended in). In the twelfth and thirteenth centuries, Icelandic authors wrote the magnificent prose narratives known as the sagas. These masterpieces were written in the Icelandic vernacular. And here's the extraordinary thing: present-day Icelanders can still read these stories, and many do. Not 'read' as in 'decipher', but actually read for enjoyment. Compare it to reading nineteenth-century English novels by the likes of Dickens, Trollope or the Brontë sisters: some words and phrases are quaint, but we take them in our stride. That's how close modern Icelandic is to its medieval form.

Of course, the language has expanded its vocabulary to keep up with the times, so the saga authors would have trouble understanding a modern newspaper. Also, there's more to language than the written word, and pronunciation has definitely changed somewhat in the interim. Nonetheless, Icelandic has remained remarkably stable for 800 years – or even 1,100, given that the first settlers are thought to have spoken a similar language.

One reason for this stasis is suggested by even a cursory glance at the map: Iceland is extremely isolated from other population centres. The distance to mainland Europe (not counting smaller islands) is roughly 1,000 kilometres, while Denmark, Iceland's colonial power and gateway to the world for centuries, is about twice that far. Until the nineteenth century, most Icelanders would go through their entire lives without encountering a foreign language.

This can't be the whole story though, because languages are prone to change even without outside influences. It takes exceptional conditions to prevent them from doing so. What is required in particular, according to sociolinguists, is that many of the people known to any one speaker should also know each other, as this maintains a consensus on linguistic norms. Icelandic society before the nineteenth century, with fewer than 50,000 people, may have been small enough to allow such close-knit

THE ICELANDIC LANGUAGE HASN'T CHANGED ALL THAT MUCH SINCE THE TIME OF THE SAGAS IN THE TWELFTH AND THIRTEENTH CENTURIES.

networks. Another glance at a map suggests an objection to this hypothesis: Iceland is very thinly inhabited, and it's very difficult to travel across, with mountains to climb and fast-streaming rivers to cross. This is true, but historians argue that in spite of these obstacles the Icelandic elites used to travel and intermingle much more than one might think: local leaders visited the yearly national council (Althing); wealthy families travelled between their various estates; elite children attended one of only two schools; and clergymen were dispatched to districts far from both their birthplace and their former parishes. The occasional volcanic eruption, moreover, forced hundreds and sometimes thousands of people to move to a different region. All these contacts may have kept the language stable – so stable in fact that even dialects were practically non-existent.

The centrality of the sagas to Icelandic culture may also have acted as a source of linguistic conformity. And there is one other explanation for Icelandic's non-development. The main source of language change, some linguists claim, is young people hanging out together. Desperate to be unlike their old folks, preferably in an annoying way, they concoct their own ways of talking as an easy means to this end. Some of this youthful lingo will survive into adulthood – and thus the local language changes.

In Iceland, however, most young people never got a chance to get the process moving, as they lived in scattered farmsteads beyond easy walking distance of each other. Apart from siblings and perhaps cousins, the young had no one to hang out with. Things would have been different at the country's two schools, but upon return to their homes, this elite minority would find themselves misunderstood or corrected whenever they let a hint of school slang pass their lips.

Isolation in a monolingual environment, strong social networks and perhaps the absence of a youth culture: these are, then, in a nutshell, the main things that made Icelandic stable for centuries. But of course the country is no longer like that. Better transport, easy communications and urbanisation have transformed Iceland over the last hundred years or so. And yet the sagas have remained accessible. Why should this be? Why do Icelanders defy the customary processes of language change?

Defiance is part of the answer. When the ideology of nationalism reached even this remote corner of Europe in the mid-nineteenth century, Icelanders immediately knew what made them a nation: their special and uncorrupted language. Leaders in the century-long fight for independence could always rely on the language to rally support. The prevailing attitude would later be summed up in the phrase *Land, þjóð og tunga, þrenning sönn og ein*, 'Land, folk and tongue, a trinity true and one'.

With the purity and stability of the language occupying such a vital place in the budding nation's self-conception, an urgent task lay ahead: to make sure that Icelandic would remain pure and stable while also serving its speakers in all aspects of modern life, from administration to zoology. This is a task that the Icelanders have been working on ever since. New words have been coined, strictly in keeping with the language of the sagas. The grammar was tidied up in a way that made the old literature more rather than less accessible than it had been. Compulsory education helped spread the new words and grammar across the country, which led to a further levelling of what few dialect differences there had been.

Until quite recently, this language policy was uncontroversial. It was widely agreed that a 'pure' Icelandic made all writing, no matter what the subject, easy to understand for a general readership. Furthermore, stability would ensure that future generations would have easy access to all the nation's literature, both old and new. And literature is important in Iceland: the country produces more new books per capita than any other nation, while Icelandic is easily the smallest language to boast a Nobel Prize winner (Halldór Laxness) in literature.

Today, however, the linguistic nationalism of Iceland has waned a little. Loanwords are no longer quite the taboo they used to be and a few grammatical changes are creeping in. Even so, awareness of these changes is high and acceptance low, so that it's quite possible that they will never become part of the standard language. The stability of Icelandic shows no signs of imminent collapse.

So if you think that English is in decline and that someone needs to do something about it, don't go thinking that the Icelanders have shown that change can be arrested. The factors that for centuries safeguarded the Icelandic language no longer exist, and have never existed in Britain. Furthermore, when those safeguards ceased to exist, they were succeeded by a peculiarly Icelandic brand of nationalism, which turned preservation of the ancient vernacular into something of a collective passion. And given the promiscuous history of English, if there's one place where a mass movement to preserve the purity of the nation's language is never going to happen, that place is Britain.

⇆ Two English words are of Icelandic origin: 'geyser', which was borrowed directly, and 'eiderdown' (from *æðardun*), via Danish or German.

💡 *Jólabókaflóð* – literally 'Christmas book flood'.

PART THREE

War and peace

Languages and politics

The history of every language is to some extent a story of politics and ideology. In different parts of Europe, egalitarianism (Sweden), pacifism (Norway) or pragmatism (Luxembourg) have played a role in shaping the way that people speak. Elsewhere, regionalism (Frisian/Scots) and separatism (Catalan) have made a huge impact, as of course have war and political repression (Serbo-Croatian; Belarusian).

14

The democratic language

Norwegian

Most Norwegians speak Norwegian and write Norwegian. While this may sound like a truism of the first order, it is in fact false. For there is no such thing as 'Norwegian', neither as a written language nor as a spoken one.

To start with the latter: the Norwegians simply have no local equivalent of the Queen's English. Every last one of them speaks a regional dialect. If you sign up for a few lessons in Norwegian before visiting the country, what you're most likely to hear on your course CD is Standard Eastern Norwegian. Which is so named for a reason – you won't find anyone from the west of Norway speaking that way. Not at home, not at work, not even on TV, because even newsreaders and actors tend to stick to their own regional pronunciation. The advice of the official *Språkråd* (Language Council) is simply: follow the habits of your own region. As a result, Norwegians understand a rich tapestry of accents. No matter whether a Norwegian says *eg, e, i, ig, je, jæ, jæi, jeg, æ, æg, æi* or *æig*, it will be understood that 'I' is what is meant. Such flexibility is admirable, but it's tough for the foreign language learner.

As relaxed and tolerant as the Norwegians are towards their vernacular, when it comes to the written language they are surprisingly rigid and combative. No peaceful coexistence of various dialects here, but instead a protracted and at times passionate struggle between all sorts of varieties.

The core of the controversy can be summed up in one question: how Danish should Norwegian be? This issue has been hotly contested for some two hundred years. In 1814 Norway broke away from Denmark, becoming effectively an independent nation, though full and official independence didn't come until 1905. But there was a problem. Under Danish rule, the Norwegian language, which in the Middle Ages had set the tone in all of Northern Europe, had been squeezed into a tight corner. Those who could write, wrote in Danish. In fact, those who wanted to achieve anything at all had to do so in Danish.

The newly autonomous Norway thus faced the difficult choice of deciding how to write. There was no standard Norwegian language. The vocabulary of the existing dialects just wasn't up to the task of national governance, higher education and lofty prose. And Danish? Now, be serious – surely the independent Norwegians weren't going to write in *Danish*? The logical compromise was a hybrid form. But exactly how to hybridise the opposing elements was far from clear. Danish with Norwegian pronunciation? The dialect of the capital, supplemented with Danish loanwords? The less Danish-influenced Norwegian of the provinces, bolstered by invented words?

This question still has no single answer. In fact, as many as four answers are presently in circulation – two official and two dissenting. The most common official version is the *Bokmål* ('Book Tongue') which, in turn, has various gradations, on a scale ranging from 'moderate' (more Danish) to 'radical' (less so). Equally official is *Nynorsk* ('New Norwegian'), which is closer to the dialects that most people speak. Strangely enough though,

A TYPICALLY NORWEGIAN WORD IS UTEPILS, A LAGER DRUNK IN THE OPEN AIR. BEER IS OF THE ESSENCE, SUNSHINE ISN'T.

it is much less common, being used most frequently in the west of the country. At school, Norwegian children learn both official languages, with priority given to one in some places, and the other elsewhere. The aforementioned Language Council is in charge of both.

In opposition to these options can be heard the rumblings of rebellious minorities. These, paradoxically enough, emerged as a result of government attempts to merge the two official varieties gradually into a single *Samnorsk* ('Common Norwegian'). That endeavour, now abandoned, aroused dissatisfaction at both ends of the spectrum.

In one corner is a fairly small, not overly influential but relatively militant lobby that advocates *Høgnorsk* ('High Norwegian'). This is similar to Nynorsk, but even more similar to its predecessor, the *Landsmål* ('the country's language'), which was the variety of Norwegian created by the Romantic poet Ivar Aasen in the nineteenth century, based on what he saw as the most unspoilt, traditional dialects.

In the other corner is *Riksmål* – 'the language of the kingdom', or 'national language' as it likes to be known. In a sense, those who favour *Riksmål* are just as traditional as their opponents, in that they too are oriented towards the past, but in their case the nostalgia is for the Danish standard language, known in Danish as *Rigsmål*. Compared to the proponents of High Norwegian, they have a larger following and more prestige, even boasting a respectable counterpart to the Language Council, the Norske Akademi, which is composed of conservative individuals of quite some stature.

Of course, systematic differences in spelling are not entirely unheard of in English either: words such as 'labour', 'theatre', 'travelling', 'axe' and 'catalogue' are spelt differently on the other side of the Atlantic. But the Norwegians, living side by side on one shore of the ocean, also manage to have two official sets of spellings (plus some unofficial sets), with differences so substantial that there are even Norwegian–Norwegian dictionaries. Confusion? You could also call it freedom of choice. Norwegian is a democratic language.

⇄ A handful of English words are borrowed from modern Norwegian: 'krill', 'fjord', 'ski', 'lemming', 'slalom'. Early Norwegian (Norse) provided many more, including 'they', 'get' and 'egg'.

💡 *Døgn* – a period of 24 hours, a day including its night. Dutch *etmaal* and Polish *doba* have the same meaning. And English might consider its need for the word *utepils*, a lager drunk in the open air.

15

Two addresses to the people of Belarus

Belarus(s)ian

Our glorious nation has two official languages. One is Russian, the language of our great Slavic brother, with its exalted history and illustrious literature. The other is Belarussian, a primitive peasant dialect transformed in 1933 by eminent scholars from the USSR into an acceptable vehicle for written communication, well suited to those who find real Russian too difficult. Thanks to the efforts of our devoted socialist scholars, even education was made possible in Belarussian, in anticipation of the great moment when all Belarussians would master the true Russian language.

But, Compatriots! There are traitors in our midst, in our beloved fatherland, and traitors all around us, who spread their poison via the foreign media that bombard us night and day. There are people – no, *scorpions* – who claim that they – and only they – speak and write the true Belarussian language. Disgrace! They rely on a tattered book from 1918 by the linguistic traitor

Bronislaw Adamovich Tarashkevich. Disgrace! This Tarashkevich was born in Lithuania and was a member of parliament in Poland. Need I say more? Was he even a true Belarussian? Not for nothing was the rat Tarashkevich exterminated by our great father Stalin in the Great Purge of 1938!

Compatriots! The language of the scorpions, this so-called *Tarashkevitsa*, bears the blatant marks of his treachery. He tore Belarussian from its Russian roots and forced it into the inferior Polish mould. Yes, his ragged book from 1918 appeared, of all things, in the Latin alphabet of the West earlier than in the Cyrillic of our Russian brethren. Had Tarashkevich achieved his aims, Belarussians would now be writing in the alphabet of the capitalist exploiters, of the imperialistic NATO, of the Poles, the pornographers and the homosexuals.

Compatriots! Thanks to our beloved leader Aleksandr Lukashenko, our fatherland maintains the closest possible ties of friendship and loyalty with our Russian brothers, with their superior language and with the pure Slavic Cyrillic alphabet. Let us defend these achievements with our lives! Long live Lukashenko! Long live the Russian language! Death to the Belarussian of the traitors!

Friends —

We have long been oppressed. Until 1990, we were suppressed by the Politburo in Moscow. Today we are suppressed by our own rulers in Minsk, by the dictator Lukashenka – friend of the Russians, enemy of his own people and of our language.

The treacherous Lukashenka has again made Russian an official language of our country, ostensibly alongside our own Belarusian, but in truth over and above it. On top of this, he refuses to let go of *Narkamawka*, the Belarusian of the black Soviet years. In 1933 the people's commissars in Moscow tarnished – no, *perverted* – the language of our forefathers by casting it in the mould of Russian. To be sure, Russian is a rich, mellifluous language, closely related to ours. But it is not ours. Any attempt to make Belarusian look more Russian is a cowardly attack on our heritage, on our independence, on our national pride.

We, all Belarusians, have the patriotic duty to hold fast to the standards for spelling, vocabulary and grammar set by Branislaw Adamavich Tarashkyevich, whom we have recognised as the father of modern Belarusian ever since he published his Belarusian school grammar in 1918. There, he described the good – the *classic* – Belarusian. The language spoken and written by intelligent, modern, democratic Belarusians. The language that should be spoken by our leaders and our teachers. *That* is our language – not Russian, nor (perhaps even worse) that pseudo-Russian hybrid, *Narkamawka*.

Friends, our prospects are bright. The Belarusian intelligentsia love their language. They write their books in the classic language. And our fellow countrymen in the diaspora, too, love our classic Belarusian. Only Lukashenka and his cronies prevent this language from acquiring the status it deserves: that of national language, the *only* official language, in all of Belarus.

And friends, do not allow yourselves to be confused by the fact that all Belarusians understand each other, no matter which language they speak or write. Do not be swayed by the fact that even Russians can understand our language. The point is this: we Belarusians are a people. And a people deserves its own language. One language, and not two half languages, like the Norwegians. Do we want Belarus to start looking like Norway? Never! And so we say: long live the singular, classic Belarusian!

....

🛈 *Talaka* – voluntary collective work in the interest of the neighbourhood. Not a communist invention, but an old tradition.

16

Kleinsteinish and its neighbours

Luxembourgish

There was once a green and fertile land – let's call it Kleinstein – where a prosperous, civilised people flourished under the benign leadership of a prince whose name was as unassuming as his people: John. The Kleinsteiners kept themselves to themselves, strove for peaceful relations with their neighbours and led a quiet and contented existence.

What was striking about the Kleinsteiners was their knowledge of languages. Amongst themselves, they spoke Kleinsteinish. But they couldn't get far with this beyond the borders of their own small country. A few people in one of the neighbouring lands spoke the same language, but the rest of the world barely knew that Kleinsteinish existed.

The Kleinsteiners decided to solve this problem in a practical way. In their first few years at school, children were taught in their own language: not only reading and writing, but also maths, science and history. Once they had mastered Kleinsteinish, their teachers stopped using it. From then on, all subjects were taught in Easternish. This was one of the biggest languages around, and because it sounded a lot like Kleinsteinish, the children were fine with it.

They could have left it at that. But directly west of Kleinstein another language was spoken, a language which was understood by many people around the world. So the Kleinsteiners decided to deliver their secondary and higher education in Westernish. Of course, the children weren't just thrown in at the deep end: they'd already had Westernish lessons during primary school, and Westernish television was popular.

As a result, most Kleinsteiners were at least trilingual. With their friends and countrymen they spoke Kleinsteinish, which felt homely and familiar. On the radio, they would generally hear Kleinsteinish, too, but their press was mostly in Easternish and the national law was written in Westernish. With foreigners,

VILL GAER IS LUXEMBOURGISH FOR 'LOVE A LOT', HERE WRITTEN ON A FLEMISH BEACH.

they would switch effortlessly to whichever suited best. This smoothed the way for commerce and gave them access to a wide range of books, since very few publishers could be bothered with Kleinsteinish. Incidentally, at school they also learnt Globish, a language used almost the world over (though their knowledge of this remained generally a tad schoolbookish). And so the Kleinsteiners lived happily ever after.

MORAL OF THE STORY: Wouldn't it be great if all of Europe were to follow Kleinstein's example? It's good to have a language that you can call your own, but why cling to it so stubbornly when a much more widely useful language is available? Of course, English is already taught all over Europe, but it's often too little and too late. Mastering a language is so much easier if you start out young and if you actually use what you learn, in geography and maths and even sports. The wise and charming folk of Kleinstein have grasped this educational principle, and look how well it has served them. And it might have served them even better had they chosen English, rather than the languages of yesterday that their neighbours happen to speak ...

Oh, and by the way, Kleinstein is not a mere figment of my imagination. The fairy tale above gives a fair description of the country whose name, just like Kleinstein's, means 'small castle': Luxembourg. Or Lëtzebuerg, as they say in Luxembourgish.

⇆ English has no loanwords from Luxembourgish.

·💡· *Verkënnen* – to gradually experience the effects of old age in body and mind.

17

Longing for languagehood

Scots and Frisian

As you're undoubtedly aware, the northernmost part of the UK is a bit different from the south. Historically different: it spent only a brief stint under Roman occupation and was late in losing its independence. Geographically different: it has a remarkable number of lochs and islands. Politically different: it has its own National Party and an overwhelming preference for the Left in general elections. Aesthetically different: its national drink is whisky, not beer. And linguistically, too, Scotland is different, for it has a *leid* that is closely related to, yet different from, English: Scots.

What you probably didn't know is that this situation is mirrored in the Netherlands. Its northernmost part spent only a brief stint under Roman occupation and was late in losing its independence to Holland; it has lots of lakes and islands; it prides itself on its *Bearenburch* liquor; and it has its own *Nasjonale Partij* and an overwhelming preference for Labour. Moreover, it has a *taal* that is closely related to, yet different from, Dutch: West Frisian, or simply *Frysk* ('Frisian'), as the Frisians call it.

In both cases you could be forgiven (though not by the natives) for asking if the regional *leid* and *taal* should not be considered dialects, rather than languages. After all, there is no denying (even by the natives) that they have a lot in common with their dominant relatives. So what do linguists say?

Strangely enough, linguists dislike the question. In their work, they make no fundamental distinction between languages and dialects. To them, Standard British English and Standard Dutch are 'prestige varieties', with their historical roots in 'elite dialects'. They would also happily refer to the dialects of English and Dutch as 'languages'. They appreciate, of course, that some languages are spoken over a wider area than others, are used in different social situations from others, are more standardised than others, et cetera. They're fully aware that English is a large language and that Scouse is rarely heard beyond Merseyside. But both are what they might call 'complete communicative systems', potentially capable of expressing the full gamut of human experience. They can be, and are, studied by linguistic scientists, because they're languages worth studying. Linguists may informally call Scouse a dialect, but this is a concession to popular usage, certainly not a value judgement.

Some speakers of Scots, Frisian and many other *leids* and *talen*, on the other hand, consider that theirs is *more* of a language than other mere dialects spoken by some of their neighbours, such as Scouse or Low Saxon, the regional language of the northeastern Netherlands and adjacent parts of Germany. The more vociferous among them will advance a whole range of reasons to support this view. None of them makes sense in terms of linguistics.

In the case of Frisian, history is always the first card to be played – 'our language is old'. But nearly all contemporary languages have a long history of uninterrupted transmission, including several that many people would classify as mere 'dialects', like Low Saxon. And it's not as if longevity were a

THE LEAVES OF THE YELLOW WATER LILY, PAINTED IN RED BETWEEN
DIAGONAL BLUE STRIPES, ARE THE TRADITIONAL SYMBOL OF FRIESLAND.
IT'S USED ON ALL THINGS FRISIAN, FROM CLOGS TO THE FRISIAN BOAT IN
THE AMSTERDAM GAY PRIDE PARADE.

prerequisite for any true language – Tok Pisin (of Papua New
Guinea), British Sign Language and Esperanto haven't been
around for long, but nobody would call them dialects. So the age
of a language/dialect is neither here nor there – and to be fair to
the champions of Scots (which diverged from English quite late
in comparison to the separation of Frisian from its neighbours),
it's not a criterion that they tend to employ.

But then there's the argument that all speakers of Frisian
can understand each other, while non speakers have trouble
understanding them – just as English people have difficulty with

Scots. This is true, but also irrelevant. If you were to drop an Oxford-bred Old Etonian into the heart of the Black Country or the streets of West Belfast he probably wouldn't be able to make head nor tail of what the people there were saying – but however rich those dialects might be, the language that's being spoken in Belfast or Dudley is nonetheless English. Militant Frisians and Scots would counter that their language is something special because it has dictionaries, grammars and a unified spelling. That is indeed somewhat special, because the great majority of the world's languages cannot boast any of these (though other regional languages in the Netherlands can). But dictionaries and grammar books don't create languages – they merely describe what's already there. So a language without a dictionary is still as much a language as Frisian.

Finally, hardcore Frisians might reason that their language has a special position because it has a longer tradition of writing and is used in more social situations than other languages within the Netherlands. The former is a dubious claim – Low Saxon is a strong competitor here. And though the latter is true, the reasoning is circular: Frisian has been *fully recognised* by the Dutch government as an *official* regional language, and it is therefore used in administrative, legal and educational contexts. Not everyone does use it, to be sure, as only about a quarter of the province's population can write Frisian, but used it is, largely in consequence of the official recognition.

So why has Frisian been elevated to the ranks of official regional languages? Here we get to the heart of the matter – it is about politics rather than linguistics. The Dutch government has recognised two other regional languages, Low Saxon and Limburgish, but not fully: they haven't been made co-official. But few Low Saxons and Limburgers are terribly bothered about this, and certainly have never come to blows with the police over the right to speak their own languages in court. The Frisians have: in

Leeuwarden, on 16 November 1951, a date which has gone down in provincial history as *Kneppelfreed* or 'cudgel Friday'. Within five years, Frisian was being used alongside Dutch in primary schools and courtrooms in the province of Friesland; official parity was granted not much later. So there you have it. Why is Frisian more of a language than Low Saxon? Because there was a riot in in Leeuwarden.

And what about Scots? Is the Scottish *leid* a real language, or isn't it? The answers range from 'Yes, of course' to 'No way', depending on the perspective you take. You'll hear 'No way' from English people who claim that their own dialect is just as different from Standard English as is Scots. They're wrong, linguists say: among the British dialects of English, those of Scotland form a cluster that's more unlike the standard than the rest. 'Yes, of course', on the other hand, is what linguists will say – not necessarily because they are persuaded by those who insist that Scots is a language rather than a dialect (though some of them are), but because they regard the distinction as a false one. What people speak is always a language, linguists argue. There is simply nothing else.

But there is a middle way. A famous German expert on minority languages, Heinz Kloss, has called Scots a 'half language'. Before the union with England, the linguistic norms of the (Germanic) language spoken by the Scots were not defined by the language of England, and the gulf between Scots and English grew with each decade of independence. After the union, as contact between the two cultures intensified, this process of divergence was reversed, with Scots falling under the ever-stronger influence of the language of the dominant partner.

From a political perspective, Scots is a 'half language' too. It has been recognised by the governments in London and Edinburgh, but it's not a co-official language and is not taught in schools, as Frisian is. It might have been, if only the Scottish had taken the trouble of rioting over the language issue. However, should Scotland become independent – which many political commentators feel is only a matter of time – then Scots may well set course for full and undisputed languagehood.

FRISIAN

....

⇆ While Frisian is close kin to English, loans from it are almost non-existent. 'Gherkin' and 'freight', both borrowed from Dutch, might be of Frisian origin. Skating enthusiasts sometimes use the word 'kluning' as an English version of Frisian *klune* for 'crossing land between two icy surfaces on skates'.

....

💡 *Tafalle* – to turn out better than expected.

SCOTS

....

⇆ Some Scots loanwords are old Germanic words that English lost and later readopted, such as *(un)canny*. Others are of Gaelic origin, such as *cairn* and *ingle*, or were borrowed from elsewhere, such as *queer* (from Low German) and *glamour* (from French).

....

💡 *Sitooterie* – literally 'sit-out-ery', a place for intimate togetherness, like a sunroom, but also a secluded corner at a party.

18

Much a-du about you, and him

Swedish

....

1967: the height of the hippie era. In America it's the Summer of Love. The Beatles, with 'Lucy in the Sky with Diamonds', are singing the praises of LSD. And, almost equally shocking, a top Swedish executive is calling for unprecedented levels of informality. Bror Rexed (53), the incoming Director-General of the *Medicinalstyrelse* (Public Health Board), announces that he intends to address all employees by their first names, and would like them to do the same for him. And he gets his way. His own first name, Bror, is the Swedish word for *brother* – how much more egalitarian can you get?

And so, ever since 3 July 1967, Rexed's name (particularly his surname, ironically enough) has been linked to the *du*-reform. *Du* in Swedish is the informal version of the English 'you', the same as it is in German, and like *tu* in French and *thou* in English (between roughly the thirteenth and eighteenth centuries, anyway). Which is not to say this was all Rexed's doing. There had been signs

OLOF PALME – THE DU PRIME MINISTER – IN 1975, FLANKED BY FELLOW
SOCIAL DEMOCRAT POLITICIANS OF GERMANY AND AUSTRIA.

already that the tide of public opinion was turning, and a short
time later even Prime Minister Olof Palme endorsed the new
trend: upon taking office in 1969 he publicly dealt with journalists
on a first-name-and-*du* basis. Nevertheless, in Sweden's collective
memory, Rexed's announcement has remained the symbolic
turning point.

It was a turning point that was overdue, because the rules
of linguistic etiquette that had been in use until then were
extremely complex. The most formal variant consisted of three
parts: *herr* ('Mr') or *fru* ('Mrs'), followed by the person's societal
position (such as doctor, count or lieutenant) and finally the
surname. If Rexed had not taken his stand, his employees would
have had to call him *herr generaldirektör Rexed*. And not as a term
of address, mind you – as we might say 'Mr Rexed' – but instead
of 'you': 'Would *herr generaldirektör Rexed* like a biscuit?'

For someone less senior, the word *herr* or *fru* could be omitted: 'Would accountant Persson mind sending the invoices this afternoon?' Another variant was the use of surname only. That, for example, was how a boss would address his subordinates: 'Did Almquist have a good weekend?' In communication with maids and servants, last names gave way to first names: 'Has Agatha emptied the chamber pots?' And among the lower classes and in the country, the typical terms were simply 'he' and, to a lesser extent, 'she': 'When will he be harvesting the rye, then?' Note that 'he' here in fact means 'you'.

All these niceties – and there were many more, such as using 'mother' when addressing an older woman (as in 'would mother Brigitta care for a cup of coffee?) – called for real precision. Mistakes were easily made, superiors quick to take offence. Swedes had to keep careful tabs on whose position or rank had changed, so as not to address as 'lieutenant' the newly promoted captain. (If ever there was a need for LinkedIn...) Only spouses and lovers had it easy: they could simply call each other *du*. So could friends, but not until they had shared a so-called '*du*-drink'. These exceptions aside, *du* was acceptable with children only, and of course with people for whom one had no respect.

Little wonder the Swedes had long toyed with the idea of reform. In the early twentieth century the word *ni*, previously used only as the plural of 'you', had enjoyed a measure of popularity as a formal singular, equivalent to *vous* in French. However, because its use aroused the suggestion that the addressee had no title, it was seen as insufficiently respectful. Another strategy was to avoid second-person pronouns entirely, by invoking cumbersome formulations like 'Would a biscuit be permitted?' instead of 'Would you like a biscuit?' But this was unwieldy, and even came to be seen as impolite.

When the revolution came, it came fast. In the early sixties, prudence still reigned. But by the close of the decade, even the prime minister had been *du*'d, like anyone off the street. Only the royal family remained out of range.

And now? Nobody longs for a return to the old system, but the informal pronoun, *du*, seems to be losing ground to *ni*, its more formal counterpart. Gradually, these two words have come to symbolise opposing visions of society. Progressive Swedes do not like *ni*. It points to 'the return of the class society', writes the social-democratic councillor Britta Sethson on her blog *Nyabrittas*. As she sees it, this practice has become mandatory in shops solely because 'employees should be made to feel, in their very bones, that they are just a little inferior'.

More conservative Swedes, by contrast, have had enough of *du*. For writer Lena Holfve, the entire first name kerfuffle is an expression of misplaced egalitarianism, while a writer going by the *nom de blog* of Bencio de Uppsala advocates a more widespread deployment of *ni*, or *ni-reformen*, as he calls it: 'In countries still bearing traces of civilisation, the option always exists of varying the degree of intimacy by way of word choice.' The etiquette consultant Magdalena Ribbing, more radically, recommends discarding second-person pronouns altogether, so as not to offend anyone. But this, as Swedish history has shown, is an untenable solution.

And the second-person singular is not the only pronoun to have become an ideological battleground in Sweden. Most European languages distinguish a feminine and masculine form: in Swedish it's *hon* for 'she', *han* for 'he'. Traditionally, the masculine form has been the default option (as in 'the reader must decide for himself'), but many languages are now seeking less sexist alternatives. In English, the singular *they* seems to be the favoured solution (as in 'someone left their car unlocked'), but the Swedes – or some Swedes, to be more precise – have gone one better by introducing a brand new pronoun, *hen*, meaning 'he or she'. The word seems to have been inspired by neighbouring

Finnish, which has just one third-person singular pronoun, *hän*. What is remarkable, given that pronouns are resistant to planned as opposed to spontaneous change, is that the new Swedish pronoun seems to have made headway. Indeed, the more radical gender activists even want to do away with the old pronouns *hon* and *han* altogether and use *hen* exclusively. This is maybe pushing things in Sweden, but the more moderate proposal might well prevail. In one or two decades, perhaps *han-reformen* will be established as another crucial episode in the history of Swedish social and linguistic politics, alongside Bror Rexed's *du*.

⇆ 'Moped' is a so-called portmanteau word of Swedish origin, built from *motor* ('engine') and *pedaler* ('pedals'). 'Smorgasbord' and 'angstrom' are Anglicised versions of *smörgåsbord* and *ångström*.

💡 *Lagom* – just right, neither too much nor too little, in desirable moderation. Literally, something 'in accordance with the laws'.

19

Four countries – and more than a club

Catalan

If you heard about the existence of a small nation called Grøtland, what would you expect its language to be? Grøtlandic, probably. And if you heard that Marelian was a national language spoken somewhere in a remote corner of Europe, what would you expect the country to be called? Why, Marelia of course. The answers to these questions show how closely land and language are linked in our minds. Unthinkingly, we tend to assume that, as a rule, countries and language areas coincide: Finland is where Finnish is spoken, Bulgaria is the home of Bulgarian, Portugal is for speakers of Portuguese, and so on.

But take a look at a detailed linguistic map of Europe, and the picture you will find is quite different. Whereas the political map is a mass of solid monochromatic blocks, the languages of the continent create something that's more like a multi-coloured mosaic in many places, while in other regions it resembles a floor that's been sprinkled with confetti.

Take Catalan, for example. Where is that spoken? In Catalonia, of course. That is to say, the autonomous region of Spain that the locals know as Catalunya. In all of Catalonia, then? Not quite. In the north, near the French border, lies the Aran Valley, a small region where Occitan is spoken. Occitan is much more widespread in France, but the language is not recognised there; the French constitution is adamant that France is, and shall remain, a monolingual republic. But since the Catalans know from historical experience just how infuriating it is when your own language is not recognised, they have not made the same mistake. And so Occitan – going by the name Aranese – has official status in the region.

Is it only the Catalonians who speak Catalan? Again, not quite. The language also crosses the regional borders on all sides. To the south, the region of Valencia is largely Catalan-speaking as well, though they prefer to call their language 'Valencian'. To the west, *català* is also spoken in part of the region of Aragon and in a small corner of Murcia. Over the northern Spanish border it is the vernacular of the French department of the Eastern Pyrenees, which even drew up a charter promoting Catalan (the *Charte en faveur du catalan*) in 2007 – the local authorities were less rigid than their overlords in Paris. Also over the northern border, Catalan is the sole language of the tiny principality of Andorra. (So if this microstate were to be granted EU membership, the EU would be forced to grant official European status to the Catalan language; perhaps Catalonia should start twisting a few arms.) Then there are the Balearic Islands, the Spanish archipelago most famous for Mallorca and the party island of Ibiza; Catalan is spoken there too. And further afield lies the Italian island of Sardinia, where Catalan has been spoken in the city of Alghero for over six centuries, and is still used today by about ten thousand people. (The late leader of the Italian Communist Party, Enrico Berlinguer, was a Sardinian with a Catalan surname.)

BARCELONA'S CAMP NOU STADIUM WITH THEIR FAMOUS SLOGAN –
PERHAPS EQUALLY APPLICABLE TO THE CATALAN LANGUAGE?

In short, Catalan is spoken by about eleven and a half million people in five different Spanish regions and three other countries. And, of course, in football stadiums all over Spain and Europe whenever the mighty Barcelona happen to be playing – for they are the great standard-bearers of Catalan identity, as the club slogan – *Més que un club* ('More than a club') – asserts.

But aren't Catalonia and its language an extraordinary anomaly? A nation is a collective of people who feel that they share a culture, isn't it? And if anything defines a culture, it's language, so surely elsewhere in Europe we'll find countries and languages much more closely linked than is the case in Spain. What about Italy and Italian, for example?

Well, Italy is another mixed bag. Not only is Italian to be heard in parts of Switzerland, Slovenia, Croatia and France, but Italy itself is home to a great many minorities who have long spoken languages that are not Italian. Some of these minorities live in border areas: for example, there are Occitan speakers near the Occitan-speaking part of France, Arpitan speakers near the Arpitan-speaking parts of France and Switzerland, German speakers near Austria and Switzerland, Slovene speakers near Slovenia, and Corsican speakers in Sardinia, not far from the French island of Corsica. But still other minorities live nowhere near a border. Greek was spoken in southern Italy hundreds of years before Christ, and in the toe and the heel of the boot various small communities cling stubbornly to Grico, their dialect of the old language. Also in the toe lies the village of Guardia Piemontese, where Occitan has been spoken ever since the twelfth century. Slightly north of the ankle of the boot, in the province of Campobasso, several hundred people still make use of a Croatian dialect, albeit one that's now heavily Italianised. Albanian has been spoken in about fifty southern Italian mountain towns since the Middle Ages, while two villages in Puglia speak Arpitan, which is otherwise used only in the region around Mont Blanc. Then there's Alghero, of course, which is holding on to Catalan for dear life. And let's not even get started on indigenous minority languages of Italy such as Friulian, Sardinian and Ladin, not to mention the Italian dialects.

So if the Catalan language area and Catalonia itself are not the same thing, and Italian is far from the whole story in Italy, you might ask: is there any country in Europe where the political boundaries and the linguistic boundaries are identical? Well, yes, there is: Iceland. Icelandic is the only language of Iceland, and its inhabitants are the only people in the world for whom

Icelandic is their mother tongue. And in all of Europe there's no other country that has a language that's unique to that country, and is spoken by all of its citizens.

....

⇄ 'Paella' is a Catalan dish and word. And 'aubergine' has made a long journey, from Sanskrit through Persian and Arabic to Catalan, and then on to French and ultimately English.

....

💡 *Alfabetitzar* – to teach how to read and write. A word with this meaning, often similar to the Catalan word, is present in most European languages, but English lacks it.

20

Four languages and zero goodwill

Serbo-Croatian

A language is a dialect with an army. If this cliché applies anywhere, it's in the former Yugoslavia. For most of the twentieth century, Yugoslavia was one country, with one army and one dominant language: Serbo-Croatian, the mother tongue of more than three-quarters of its population. Then, between 1991 and 2008, Yugoslavia split into seven parts, each with its own army. In three of the new countries – Slovenia, Macedonia and Kosovo – the majority of the population spoke Slovenian, Macedonian and Albanian, respectively, and these became their national languages. But each of the other four countries also claimed its own language: Croatian in Croatia, Serbian in Serbia, Montenegrin in Montenegro and Bosnian in Bosnia-Herzegovina (although the ethnic Croats in this lacerated country tend to speak Croatian, and the Serbs Serbian). In so doing, they abolished Serbo-Croatian.

Serbo-Croatian, it must be admitted, was always a bit artificial. In the mid-nineteenth century a small group of literati decided to fashion a single, standard language from the diverse South Slavic vernaculars they had used until then. In the absence of an army, the new hybrid remained primarily a literary language. It was only when Yugoslavia was created in 1918 that the reformers' dream finally came to fruition.

For English speakers, this imposition of a newly created language might sound like an odd state of affairs. Yet most European languages came about by means of a similar process. In the Middle Ages, English, too, was originally a collection of regional vernaculars. From the sixteenth century on, a written standard began to emerge, contrived by printers and learned men, but spoken by nobody. Its spoken counterpart came only later, very gradually, after centuries of reading and schooling. Thus English and Serbo-Croatian took a comparable route – it's just that English covered the route more slowly, and a few centuries earlier. And a good thing too, because it also had a greater distance to travel: speakers of dialects such as Anglo-Cornish and Geordie had a great deal more trouble understanding one another than do speakers of the different dialects that went into Serbo-Croatian.

With the disintegration of Yugoslavia, the national language must have split once more into its constituent dialects. Right?

Wrong. The old dialects live on, but they don't map onto the new languages; not by a long shot. The main dialect of former Yugoslavia, Shtokavian, is spoken in Croatia, Serbia, Montenegro and Bosnia-Herzegovina, while the two other major dialects are used only in Croatia. Insofar as linguistic diversity exists in the region, then, it is largely to be found in Croatia. In this respect, Serbia, Montenegro and Bosnia are relatively homogenous.

But people often insist on accentuating their differences from their neighbours, and in this part of the world difference is of paramount importance. For nationalist Serbs, for example, the use of the Cyrillic script is an essential distinction between their

SINCE THE WAR, THE LANGUAGE ITSELF HAS BECOME A MINEFIELD.

culture and that of the Croats, who hold fast to the Latin alphabet. (The Montenegrins and Bosnians are fairly flexible in their choice of script.) Pronunciation, vocabulary and grammar also come into play in the battle for uniqueness. While the Croats say *Europa*, the Serbs speak of *Evropa*. (This is not so extraordinary; in the Netherlands, for example – a country smaller than both Croatia and Serbia – the first two letters of 'Europe' may be pronounced in three different ways, none of which resemble the English.) For 'girl' or 'maiden', Bosnians say *djevojka*, some Croats *divojka* and some Serbs *devojka*, while Montenegrins prefer *đevojka* – spot the differences. (Similarly, 'girl' is also pronounced differently by English, American and Scottish speakers – along the lines of 'guhl', 'grrrl' and 'gurril', respectively – though this variation hides behind a single standard spelling.) Serbs call a tomato *paradajz* ('paradise'), while Croats call it a *rajčica*, derived from the word *raj* (also 'paradise'). All four groups have preferred 'he started that he sang' over 'he started to sing', but the Croats are now trying to kick the habit, because this particular construction originates from the Balkans and as far as Croatia is concerned the Balkans begin with Bosnia.

Those who have left their nationalistic-coloured glasses at home can see these machinations for what they are: political tinkering, plain and simple. Just as all English speakers can understand one another provided a dash of goodwill is thrown into the mix, so, too, can Serbs, Montenegrins, Bosnians and Croats. But if your family was massacred by your neighbour's army, goodwill is hard to find.

A language is indeed a dialect with an army – one army, that is. Once upon a time, Serbo-Croatian fitted that description. Today, it is a dialect with four armies – and so, four languages.

⇆ The word 'cravat' derives ultimately (via German and French) from the Serbo-Croatian word for Croat. The scientific unit 'tesla' is named after the Serbian inventor Nikola Tesla.

💡 *Merak* – pleasure derived from simple activities, such as spending time with friends.

PART FOUR

Werds, wirds, wurds ...

Written and spoken

Unlike English, many languages (Polish, Czech) spell their words in wonderfully systematic ways – albeit that some systems (Scots Gaelic, for example) are a little mad. However bizarre they may seem to outsiders, every language has its spelling conventions, which enable us to identify all those written in Latin script (Estonian), while even Cyrillic is not as formidable a hurdle as you may fear (Russian). As for speaking – some people seem to talk too fast (Spanish), some use dialects even their neighbours would struggle to understand (Slovene), and others sound as if they're trying to hide something (Shelta and Anglo-Romani).

21

'Háček!' – 'Bless you'

Czech

How do you spell a sneeze? This is an important question for the Czechs – after all, their name starts with one. And it's a tricky question, it seems, because all over Europe the 'ch' sound can be spelt in as many as eighteen ways: *c, ċ, ç, ĉ, č, ch, çh, ci, cs, cz, tch, tj, tš, tsch, tsi, tsj, tx* and even *k*.

So why the profusion of different spellings? In the Middle Ages, when the people of Europe began to write their languages down, they took the classical writing traditions as their starting points: Latin in Western Europe, Greek in the East. But an alphabet that is suited to one language isn't necessarily suited to another. Every language has its own particular sounds, and these are sometimes hard to represent with an existing letter.

There are five solutions to this problem.

The first is to muddle on with the old alphabet. In the oldest Czech texts, 'ch' was written as *c*. But this same *c* could also stand for the sounds 'ts' and 'k'. Not so practical, then.

Solution two, the clean-slate approach, is the most radical. In the ninth century the Slavic writers designed an alphabet

CZECH IS NO LONGER AS PURIST AS IT USED TO BE. IN DUE COURSE, THE
SPELLING WILL LIKELY CHANGE TO 'SNOBORDOVÝ KLUB'.

specially for their language: Glagolitic, which would later give
rise to Cyrillic (see p.245 for more on this). Because the 'ch' sound
is very common in the Slavic languages, it was given a separate
letter. A downside of this solution, at least in modern times, is that
it forms a major communication barrier with speakers of other
languages. How many readers recognise the name Чехия on first
glance? (It's the Russian spelling for *Chekhia*, i.e. Czech Republic.)

The other solutions use the existing Latin alphabet, but in
a creative way. For example, solution three is to recycle letters.
Present-day Czech reserves the *c* for the *ts* sound – and never
uses the letter c for the 's' or 'k' sounds, unlike many Western
European languages which do exactly that. For those sounds,

Czech uses, quite sensibly, the *s* and the *k*. It works well, even if it looks odd to us, with tsar, for example, written as *car*.

Solution four is about pairs: combining two (or more) letters to represent one sound. Modern Czech has the combination *ch*, which is used rather as in the English *loch* – with a Czech accent, of course.

Until the early fifteenth century Czech used far more of these pairs than it does today. But when Jan Hus, best known as a religious reformer, took it upon himself to rationalise the Czech spelling system, he chose solution five: special symbols above the letters, known as diacritics or diacritical marks. Without him, Czech would have no vowels with an acute accent (*á, ý*), nor would it have outlandish consonants such as *ř, š* and *ž*. In English, we call this accent a hacek, caron or inverted circumflex. The Czechs, appropriately enough, have added one to its name and call the little hook a *háček*, meaning 'little hook'.

This system, which was modified in the succeeding centuries, has since gathered quite a following in Eastern Europe. Four other Slavic languages (Slovak, Slovene, Serbo-Croatian and Sorbian) and the two Baltic languages (Latvian and Lithuanian) all show signs of a Czech influence, while the system used by linguists to render Cyrillic words in the Latin alphabet is also based on the Czech example.

⇆ The most famous Czech loanword is 'robot', coined by Karel Čapek in 1920 on the basis of a word for 'slave'. 'Semtex' is Czech, too; the name was created by merging 'Semtín' (the city where it was first manufactured) and the first syllable of 'explosive'.

💡 *Ptydepe* – coined by playwright and president Václav Havel, this has come to mean 'unintelligible jargon of some professional group'.

22

Szczęsny, Pszkit and Korzeniowski

Polish

Foreign names are often difficult to pronounce and remember. This is especially true for surnames, which tend to be longer than given names. And as all names are foreign in most parts of the world, it's a very widespread problem. Growing up in the Netherlands, I found many English names hard to pronounce, remember or even make sense of. What did *ai* and *th* stand for in Braithwaite? (Both these letter combinations are rare in Dutch and are not pronounced the English way.) Was I to pronounce 'Fforde' and 'Lloyd' with a stutter? What was I to make of the *w* and the *h* in 'Wright'? When I came to explore English literature, I discovered that the authors Maugham, Crichton and Yeats (but not Keats) were pronounced in unexpected ways, as was Graham Greene's character Cholmondeley. My hero Wodehouse, it turned out, was to be pronounced as if the name had an additional 'o', which was all the more surprising since President Roosevelt was to sound as if he had one fewer. Et cetera, et cetera.

Obviously, Brits have the reverse problem with Dutch names such as Van den Hoogenband, Schreurs, IJsseldijk, Bergkamp (yes, you do – believe me) and, of course, Cruijff. And both you and I have the occasional spot of trouble with names originating from elsewhere in Europe, such as Deshaies, Tejada, Etxeberria, Rößler, Anagnostopoulos and Øvergård, which are French, Spanish, Basque, German, Greek and Norwegian respectively.

But of all of Europe's challenging family names, Polish surnames are probably the trickiest. Why should this be? Is the Polish language more difficult to pronounce than the rest? Does it have a more erratic spelling? Or do Poles just happen to have weird names? The answer is none of the above.

Sure, it isn't easy for English (or Dutch) tongues to wrap themselves around certain Polish sounds. It has nasal vowels like French (*un bon vin blanc*), throaty fricatives like German and Scots (*Bach, loch*), a strong taste for consonant clusters like the other Slavic languages (witness Strzelecki, Ćmikiewicz, Szczęsny) and a bewildering array of subtly different 'sh' and 'ch' and 'j' sounds like – well, like few others. Yet none of this makes Polish *exceptionally* difficult. And Polish spelling, far from being erratic, is actually exemplary in its consistency. Every Polish name is pronounced the way it's spelt. No Cholmondeleys and Maughams to trip you up. And as for weird names: many Polish surnames have etymologies similar to their counterparts in English.

Most frequent of all Polish surnames is Nowak, which corresponds to Newman in English, Neumann in German, Nijman in Dutch, Novello in Italian, and so on. The second most frequent is Kowalski, a derivation of the word for 'smith', a name which is even more widespread throughout Europe, from Portugal to Russia and from Britain to Greece. Other top-twenty names include Kamiński (Stone), Zieliński (Green), Szymański (Simmons, Simpson), Kozłowski (Buck), Jankowski (Johnson) and Krawczyk (Tailor/Taylor).

Meet the Smiths (and other forgers)

Smith, the commonest of English surnames, is common
far beyond Britain – names with the same meaning are
widespread all over Europe. In Romania, the sculptor
Ion Schmidt-Faur went one better: his name translates
as 'John Smith-Smith'. The following list of European
Smiths is by no means exhaustive:

Latin - Faber (this name is now found in several countries)	*Dutch* - Smit, Desmet, Smeets
French - Lefèvre, Lefebvre	*Scandinavian* - Smed
Spanish - Herrero, Ferrero	*German* - Schmidt
Portuguese - Ferreira	*Frisian* - Smedema
Italian - Ferrari, Ferraro, Ferrelli	*Scottish Gaelic* - MacGowan
Romanian - Faur	*Breton* - Goff
Polish - Kowal, Kowalski	*Greek* - Siderakis
Czech - Kovař	*Estonian* - Sepp
Slovenian - Kovač	*Finnish* - Seppänen
Ukrainian - Kovalenko	*Latvian* - Kalējs
Hungarian - Kovács	*Lithuanian* - Kalvis
Russian - Koeznetsov	*Georgian* - Mchedlidze
Armenian - Darbinyan	*Turkish* - Demirci

So what makes it so hard for us to get a handle on Polish
surnames? The main reason is that Polish spelling, though
consistent, follows a logic all its own. Take the seemingly
innocuous name Lech Walesa. To begin with, this is an
international misspelling, for in Polish it's Lech Wałęsa, with
a cross-bar through the *l* and a little tail underneath the *e*. If
you had never heard the name, you might pronounce Lech as
'leck' or 'letch' and Walesa/Wałęsa as 'wah-lay-sa' or perhaps
'way-lee-za'. Having heard the name on the news, you're more

SIMPLIFIED SPELLING FOR THE ARSENAL GOALKEEPER. HE IS MORE
PROPERLY SZCZĘSNY.

likely to say 'lek vah-len-sa' or 'lek vah-wen-sa'. The latter is not
a bad approximation. But the 'ch' of Lech is actually closer to
the 'ch' of 'loch', while the ę of Wałęsa is not pronounced 'en',
but more like the first *i* in *lingerie* (French, not Anglo-American
pronunciation). So, the *ch* and the *w* represent different sounds
than in English, while the *ł* represents our 'w' and the *ę* stands
for a rather unfamiliar sound.

If something as straightforward as Walesa is so full of surprises,
what are we to make of names that look puzzling to begin with?
For instance, that of Arsenal goalkeeper Wojciech Szczesny (or
rather, Szczęsny)? Having learnt from previous mistakes, we now
know that the *w* should be 'v', the *ch* sounds as in *loch* and the *ę* as
in 'lingerie'. But there are fresh challenges here. The *c* is not an
's', but should be seen in combination with the *i* and pronounced
more or less 'tch'. The first two letters of the surname, *sz*, are
regularly pronounced as 'sh', while the next two letters, *cz*, are
sounded as in our word Czech, that is as 'tch' - but a slightly
different 'tch' from the one in Wojciech. So the name Szczęsny

begins with 'shch' – for us a near-impossible combination, but in Polish a common one. There's a major Polish city called Szczecin, for instance, and the surname of a successful Polish middle-distance runner even adds another consonant to the cluster: Adam Kszczot. Indeed, 'shch' is so frequent in Slavic languages that the Cyrillic alphabet has a special character for it: щ.

There are several other complications to Polish. It has two different varieties of a j-like sound, one spelt as *dź*, the other either as *dż* or as *rz*. (Polish pronunciation is predictable on the basis of spelling, but the reverse statement is not entirely true.) Besides *ę*, it has another nasal sound, written as *ą* but pronounced like the *o* in 'long', only more nasal. It has two ways of writing the 'ny' sound of *canyon* and *señor*, namely *ń* and *ni*. Many of these spelling rules are not shared by any other national language, Slavic or otherwise, so it's fair to say that for any outsider it is indeed hard to pronounce Polish words correctly. And with most Polish words, the need never arises. But names are a different matter, of course, especially now that half a million Poles live in Britain.

Poles have known for a long time that outsiders struggle to pronounce their names. Which is why, in the past, some of them restyled themselves. Denis Matyjaszek decided to use his mother's surname and became the Labour politician Denis MacShane. Mirosław Pszkit chose to become Miroslaw Denby-Ashe, a decision that may later have furthered the career of his daughter Daniela in *EastEnders*. And Józef Korzeniowski simply converted an anglicised version of his middle name into a surname. We know him as Joseph Conrad.

....

⇆ The 'mazurka' is named after a Polish region, Mazowsze. 'Horde' is originally a Turkic word which reached English through Polish, where the initial 'h' was added.

....

💡 *Kilkanaście* – literally 'some-teen'; an unspecified number from thirteen to nineteen.

114

23

Broad and slender tweets

Scots Gaelic

Scots Gaelic is an endangered language, but Scotland's community of texters, tweeters and users of other social media are doing their bit to adapt it to the modern world. Their focus is often on the wilder idiosyncrasies of Gaelic spelling, which is no bad thing, you might think. But many guardians of the old ways can see little benefit in what's happening. George McLennan, who has written extensively on the language, has complained about this 'cavalier approach to spelling' and considers that texting has 'negative implications for the language'. Gaelic spelling may be complex, he argues, but it's based on a useful system.

He has a point. There is indeed a certain logic to it. But I would argue that Gaelic spelling is flawed. It's wasteful, arcane and outdated. 'Wasteful' may seem a peculiar adjective to use, so let me explain. Many languages have more sounds (phonemes, to use the technical term) than there are letters in their alphabet. English, for instance, has 24 consonant phonemes, whereas its alphabet has only 21 consonant characters. Of these, *c*, *q* and *x* do not, in English at least, add any real value, since the phonemes they represent are already covered by other characters: c by s and k, q by kw and x by ks. (Other languages, such as Czech, Albanian and Portuguese, have put these letters to better use, to represent different sounds.) That leaves English with 18 useful consonant characters. The other 6 consonant phonemes are formed by means of combinations: *ng*, *ch* and *sh* represent one consonant sound each, while *th* represents two different sounds (as in *bath* and *bathe*). The letter *s* combines with *i* or *u* to represent the consonant one hears in the middle of *measure* and *vision*.

Gaelic, on the other hand has no fewer than 30 consonant sounds, so the Scots of old, the creators of the current spelling, would have done well to use all the 21 consonants of the available alphabet and think up clever ways to represent the missing 9. What they did instead was to jettison *j*, *k*, *q*, *v*, *w*, *x*, *y* and *z*, leaving them with just 13 consonants. Now that's what I call wasteful. The move resulted in a staggering challenge: how do you represent 30 different consonant phonemes with a mere 13 letters?

One way of making up the shortfall was to make maximum use of the letter *h*, a consonant rarely used in isolation but frequently employed as a means of changing the pronunciation of the preceding consonant. This is of course similar to the English practice of writing *th*, *sh* and *ch*, which do not sound at all like a *t*, an *s* or a *c* followed by an *h*. If Gaelic had used all of the available 21 consonant letters, this method alone could have generated more than enough combinations to write all the required consonant phonemes. But with only 13, that's not possible.

And that's not the end of the wastefulness. Several combinations, such as *bh* and *mh*, stand for the same sound (in this case 'v'). What's more, the combination *fh* is silent. And *lh*, *nh* and *rh* do not exist at all, so the letter *h* could have been made to work a bit harder.

Defenders of the old ways could, with some justification, argue that there's a grammatical method to this apparent madness. As in Welsh, consonants in Gaelic are often altered under certain grammatical conditions, and in Gaelic, many of these changes show up as an added *h*. Take the word *meud* ('size' or 'amount'), for example; *mheud* is one of its variants, and in this form its initial 'm' sound becomes a 'v' sound. But why not write *veud*, if that's how it's pronounced? Two other Celtic languages, Manx Gaelic and Welsh, have chosen to give the 'v' sound a letter of its own, and they are none the worse for it.

But deployment of the letter *h* is not the only way in which Scots Gaelic makes up for the shortage of consonants. Many of its consonant sounds occur only when one of the neighbouring vowels is 'slender' (*e* or *i*, which represent the sounds of English words like *get*, *hit* and *breeze*) while others occur only when having 'broad' neighbours (*a*, *o* and *u*, sounding as in the English *last*, *rock*, *tone* and *ruse*).* Accordingly, a spelling rule was devised: each and every consonant (or group of consonants), except at the beginning and end of a word, must be enclosed either by two slender vowels or by two broad vowels. Depending on this, the consonant is pronounced 'the slender way' or 'the broad way' (except if it belongs·to the small group of one-size-fits–all consonants that have only one version). This way, the scarcity of consonant letters is largely solved: *d*, *l*, *ch*, *dh* and many other consonants can represent two different sounds, and the neighbouring vowels clarify which one is to be chosen.

But this solution comes at a price. It saddles the language with a huge number of silent vowels. Take the word for 'metal', which was borrowed from English and which sounds more or less like 'metilt'. As the *t* has to be pronounced 'the broad way' (namely

---

* The reason for these correlations is that certain tongue movements are easier than others. The same habits of the tongue explain why the Romans at some point changed the pronunciation of the *c*. The word *circus*, for instance, used to be pronounced as 'keerkoos', but the 'k' before the 'ee' became an 's', and their 'seerkoos' ultimately became the English 'sirkus'.

GETTING DOWN WITH N JU – GAELIC-LANGUAGE PUNKS, OI POLLOI.

as an English *t* rather than an English *ch*, which is the 'slender' version), two *a*s have to be added: *meatailt*. This is one of the reasons why Gaelic words are often so long on paper. (Admittedly, modern loans do not always conform to the rule. The word for 'television', which sounds like its English equivalent, is spelt as *teilebhisean*, which, as the *t* is followed by a 'slender' vowel, ought to be pronounced more like *chelevision*, but isn't.)

And there's yet another downside. Like English, Gaelic has quite a few diphthongs, which are vowel pairs that produce a distinctive sound: *ao, ai, eu*, and so on. As a result, it is often unclear whether a vowel is to be read as part of a diphthong or as a modifier of a neighbouring consonant. *Meatailt* is a case in point: are the *ea* and *ai* diphthongs or are they representations of *e* and *i*, with the *a*'s thrown in to broaden the *t*? And that's without taking into account the oddity that some vowel pairs are not diphthongs at all. The *ei* combination, for instance, is entirely gratuitous: it might as well be written as a simple *e*.

It gets worse. For one thing, several consonants are rather inconsistent: the letter *d* occasionally wants to be pronounced as 'k'; the *n* every once in a while insists on sounding as 'r'; and the *s* in some places demands the pronunciation 'st'. Other consonants, on the other hand, are silent. They weren't in the past, but pronouncing them nowadays would be as silly as pronouncing the *gh* in *thought*. Worse yet: many of these silent consonants are accompanied by one or two silent vowels, because they have to observe the broad-or-slender rule, whether silent or not. And as if that weren't enough, silent letters get added to words that have been imported from elsewhere. One such word is the English *quay*. It's pronounced the British way, 'key', so in Gaelic the spelling *ci* would make perfect sense. But it has been decided that the correct spelling is *cidhe*. Probably because it looks more 'olde' and more Celtic. And sometimes it's even worse, when the spelling is changed to make it square with ancient pronunciation. The word for 'foot' (the measure, not the body part), for instance, used to be spelt *troidh*, but this was altered to *troigh* because a long time ago it was pronounced with a *g*; today, however, it's pronounced as 'troy', which is how it was pronounced when the change was made.

Scots Gaelic spelling, a logical system? Compared to English, yes, but that's hardly an achievement. The old 'system' is way past its best-by date. If we want Scots Gaelic to survive – and who doesn't? – we'd be well advised to think of the young people who are using it *today*. In Gaelic: *an-diugh*. Or as tweeters and texters would have it: *n ju*.

....

⇆ 'Loch', 'clan', 'bard' and 'plaid' are all Scots Gaelic loans, as is 'bog' and, of course, 'whisky' (from Gaelic *uisce beatha*). It's often hard to distinguish between Scottish and Irish Gaelic loans.

....

💡 *Bourach* – a particularly Scottish mess that you might be tempted to suggest defines the Gaelic language.

24

Learning your A to Я

Russian

Few people study Ancient Greek nowadays, yet most of us are familiar with a few letters of the Greek alphabet. If you've studied science of any sort, you'll be on good terms with several, because the terminology of the sciences is peppered with symbols taken from the Greek language. The best-known example is of course π (pi), the mathematical constant that connects the diameter and the circumference of a circle. But this is just the tiniest tip of the iceberg. There's μ (mu), which stands for the metric prefix *micro*, as in μm for micrometre or one millionth of a metre. Statisticians use the χ^2 (chi-squared) test when assessing the significance of correlations. Any respectable formula sports at least one Δ (delta) for 'change' or Σ (sigma) for 'summation'. The capital Ω (omega) is ubiquitous in electronics as the symbol for ohm, the unit of resistance. And so on, from unremarkable Γ (gamma) to Chinese-looking Ξ (xi). Of the 24 letters of the Greek alphabet, only omicron is hardly ever used, because it's the spitting image of our own 'o' and thus too similar to zero. All the others dot the pages of maths and science textbooks and journals.

But is this knowledge of any use outside academia? To an extent, yes. For one thing, it makes your holiday in Greece a little easier: road signs and station names aren't quite so daunting when you know that a Δ is a *D* and a Σ is an *S*. And it will also be of considerable assistance in Russia, a country in which – unlike in tourism-dependent Greece – 'bi-alphabetical' signs are something of a rarity.

But the Russian alphabet is Cyrillic, isn't it? Yes it is. But no fewer than 24 of its letters are derived from Greek capitals, so knowing your Greek letters will help a great deal. And half of them are dead easy, as this list will show. (The letters have been placed in an order based on the Latin alphabet; the usual Latin transcriptions are given in parentheses.)

A (A)	identical to Greek A
E (YE)	identical to Greek E; this is one of four Cyrillic vowels preceded by a 'y' sound
Φ (F)	identical to Greek Φ
Γ (G)	identical to Greek Γ
K (K)	nearly identical to Greek K
M (M)	identical to Greek M
O (O)	identical to Greek O
Π (P)	identical to Greek Π
P (R)	identical to Greek P
T (T)	identical to Greek T
X (KH/CH)	identical to Greek X
У (U)	very similar to Greek Y

The other half of the Greek-derived Cyrillic letters have some surprises in store:

B (V)	same shape as Greek, but pronounced as 'v' (as in Modern Greek).

Б (B)   derived from Greek B, and with the same sound as in
        Ancient Greek, i.e. 'b'.

C (S)   derived from the Greek Σ (s), though the right-indentation
        was transmogrified into a crescent or 'lunate sigma'.

Д (D)   derived from Greek Δ, with two little feet added; in some
        fonts, the Д has a sharp top, as in Greek.

Ё (YO) same origin as E, with dots added (though often omitted).

Э (E)   same origin as E. In older Cyrillic, it used to be Є.

H (N)   derived *not* from Greek H, but N.

Л (L)   derived from Greek Λ. Like Д, it sometimes occurs in a
        pointy shape more similar to the classical form.

И (I)   derived from Greek H, which in classical times sounded like
        the 'e' in *bed*, but later changed to the the 'i' as in *machine*.

Й (Y)   same origin as И ; this stands for our Y as a consonant (as
        in *boy*), rather than as a vowel (as in *myth*).

З (Z)   derived from Greek Z (zeta), it looks a bit like an old-
        fashioned Latin z, but is easily confused with Э.

Ю (YU) derived from a Greek I and O joined together – though this
        description cuts some historical corners.

In all, there are 33 letters in the Cyrillic alphabet – or in the Russian version of it, to be exact (other languages have slightly different sets). The Greek alphabet can help us to memorise 24 of them, as we've seen. That leaves just nine, which can be divided into three groups. There's nothing for it but to learn these by heart.

Group 1: *yeri* and the *yers*:

Ы (Y)   called *yeri*, this letter is conventionally transcribed as Y
        (in its vowel role), but it really represents a sound
        somewhere in between the *i* of *machine* and the German
        'ü'. Its pronunciation is a notorious hurdle for Western
        European learners of Russian.

Ь (')   to speak good Russian, one needs to learn when and how
        to pronounce this 'soft sign'; tourists can safely ignore it.

Ъ   the 'hard sign' is even more marginal, and is usually left out when transcribing Russian into the Latin alphabet. The soft and hard signs together are called the two *yers*.

Group 2: sibilants (hissing noises)

This is where things get really Slavic. Most of these letters are derived from the Glagolitic alphabet (see p.245).

Ц (TS)   as in *tsunami*. In many languages 'ts' is perceived as one sound. In German it's written as *z*, in Czech and Hungarian as *c*.

Ч (CH)   as in *chicken*.

Ж (ZH)   sounds like the middle consonant in *measure*.

Ш (SH)   as in *bush* or *shirt*.

Щ (SHTSH) in spite of the five-character transcription, in modern Russian it sounds like a long 'sh', as in *bush-shirt*.

Group 3: the 'mirrored R'

Я (YA)   as in *yard*. Though at least two Cyrillic letters (Э and Ю) underwent mirroring at some point in history, Я did not originate as a mirrored R, but developed out of the older Ѧ. This is the last letter of the Russian alphabet.

АННА КАРЕНИНА

РОМАНЪ

ГРАФА

Л. Н. ТОЛСТАГО

ВЪ ВОСЬМИ ЧАСТЯХЪ

A CLASSIC LITERATURE AWAITS ....

There, we're done. And not just for capitals, because the good news about Cyrillic is that nearly all of its lower-case letters are miniature versions of the capitals. And even the exceptions are child's play: the small A is an a, the small E an e, with or without dots. (We don't realise it, but Latin letters are much harder in this regard: compare D and d, G and g, r and R.)

But there's bad news too: Cyrillic *italics* are a challenge, and handwriting is worse than in our Latin script. The worst of all is the *d*. It comes in several varieties:

standard capital Д, lower-case д (but pointier varieties exist)
italic capital *Д*
italic lower-case *д* (similar to δ, which is, however, a variety of the б)
handwritten capital: *Д*
handwritten lower-case: *д*

Fortunately, of the written words you'll come across in Russia, the great majority will be in standard type. Nearly all signs saying Омск, Санкт-Петербург, Эрмитаж and Екатеринбург will now be legible to you. And you'll even understand useful words such as паспорт, аэропорт, туалет, метро, музей, театр, киоск, ресторан, меню, чизбургер and суши.

You'll be able to navigate much more easily the largest country on earth by learning just 33 letters, most of which, on closer inspection, turn out not to be so hard after all. A big reward for just a little effort, I'd say.

....

⇆ Most Russian loanwords are directly related to Russian culture: 'tsar', 'intelligentsia', 'vodka', 'dacha', 'apparatchik'. More general borrowings are 'steppe', 'mammoth' and 'taiga'.

....

💡 *Beloruchka* – literally 'white-hand person'; somebody who shirks dirty work.

25

Pin the name on the language

Following the clues

....

Since the fall of the Wall and the expansion of the EU, passports, manuals, labels and food packaging have been overflowing with texts in all sorts of languages. The names of the different languages are not always given, and this can offer the linguaphile an interesting challenge – and sometimes a tough one, too. Take a sentence like *Ööbik võib laulda terve öö ehast koiduni* – what on earth can that be?

The first clue is obvious: the text is in the Latin alphabet. This rules out at least ten European languages. It can't be Greek, whose alphabet is familiar. It also can't be Armenian, which you can see in the chapter called Հայերեն բառասույթ, nor Georgian, with its distinctive curly characters. And it can't be any of the languages that use the Cyrillic script, discussed in the previous chapter, and which is used not just in Russian but also in Bulgarian, Macedonian, Ukrainian, Ossetian, Serbo-Croatian (in part, anyway) and Belarusian.

Most European languages use the Latin alphabet. But they too betray their identity, if you know where to look. They all have special characters, accents (diacritics) or letter combinations. To spot the difference between written languages, the list of tell-tale signs below should suffice – at least, as long as you don't find yourself up against such rarities as Sorbian or Sami.

The following distinctive characters and punctuation marks are unique (or near enough) to one particular language.

þ or 'thorn' – Icelandic.

ß – German (not used by the Swiss, who replaced it with ss).

ı, İ The small i with no dot and the capital I with a dot – Turkish (though Irish occasionally prefers its i's dotless).

¡ ¿ Upside-down question marks and exclamation marks (¡Viva España! ¿Por qué?) – unmistakeably Spanish.

A colon in the middle of a word (as in S:t for a saint's name) – usually Swedish (sometimes Finnish – but Finnish looks generally different).

å, ä – Frequent use of å and ä is Swedish, again.

œ (o and e fused together) – French, as in œnologie (the study of wine).

Diacritics that you can't help but notice are the lines across, above or below the letters.

đ – unique to Serbo-Croatian (insofar as it uses the Latin alphabet).

ħ – exclusively Maltese (as are the dotted letters ċ and ġ).

ł – only Polish (and Sorbian, which we're ignoring here).

ē, ī – typically Latvian, which also uses the cedilla in unexpected places: ķ, ļ, ņ and even above the lower-case g: ģ.

Some relatively familiar symbols, like the dot (i), acute accent (é), circumflex (ê), tilde (ñ) and the 'Scandinavian ring' (å) also turn up occasionally in less familiar places.

ė – Lithuanian is the only language to put a dot on top of its e.

ŵ – This is seen only in Welsh. Also unique to Cymraeg are words that start with a double f or double d.

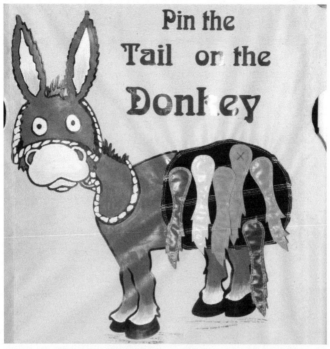

THE LANGUAGE VARIANT IS NOT SO DIFFERENT ...

ĉ, ĝ, ĥ, ĵ , ŝ – typical of the artificial language Esperanto.

ã – If there's a tilde on top of an *a*, you're looking at Portuguese.

ŕ, ĺ – Slovakian is the only European language that puts an acute accent on an *r* or an *l*. Not to be confused with the capital letter *i* with an acute accent, as in *Íslenska* (Icelandic for 'Icelandic').

ů – that is, the letter *u* with a 'Scandinavian ring', can only be Czech. Needless to say, the Czechs would prefer it be called a 'Czech ring'.

Then there are a number of less familiar characters.

l·l – a dot above the line between two *l*'s is Catalan.

ă, ţ – a loop on the *a* is typically Romanian, as is a comma under the *t*. Don't call this a 'cedilla' if you're within earshot of a Romanian. Here's a cedilla: *façade*. Quite different.

ő, ű – *o* or *u* topped with a cross between the 'German' umlaut and the 'French' acute accent is a dead giveaway for Hungarian.

į, ų – some languages like to give certain vowels a little tail. Of these, the *į* and *ų* are exclusively Lithuanian – just like the *ė*.

English is the only European language with no diacritical marks, with the exception of occasional loanwords, and even in those cases they are often omitted.

Other languages are recognisable thanks to frequent letter combinations that never, or at least rarely, turn up elsewhere.

zz – if you see double *z* between two vowels, you're probably looking at Italian (*ragazzi!*). If, in addition, some of the words end in a vowel that has a grave accent (*à, ì, ò*), it's definitely Italian (*caffè*).

ij – there's a good chance it's Dutch, especially if it stands in front of a consonant, though it could be Latvian. But in the case of a double capital letter, the case is closed: *IJsselmeer*.

c'h – this can only be Breton, which also uses the 'Spanish' *ñ*.

çh – surefire sign of Manx.

While others can be identified from odd letter patterns.

Is the *q* not typically followed by a *u* and does the letter *ë* turn up frequently? You're looking at Albanian. Case in point: the country's name, *Shqipëria*.

Is the circumflex used on the letters *a, e, o* and *u*, but not on *i, y* or *w*? That would be Frisian, spoken in Friesland – or (in Frisian) Fryslân.

Do many words in mid-sentence start with a capital letter and also use the letter *ë*? You're talking Luxembourgish.

If the letters *ð* and *ø* are both present, it's Faroese.

If both *å* and *ø* are used and there are double consonants at the end of a word, that's Norwegian. No double final consonants? Danish.

If the combinations *tx* and *tz* occur regularly, and not a single word starts with r, it's Basque.

If both the double *ä* and the double *y* are present, it must be Finnish: *älykkyysosamäärä* ('IQ').

If some words have a grave accent on the last letter (*daventà*) and many words end in *s*, it's got to be Romansh.

128

If the second letter of a word is often *h*, preceded by *b*, *d* or *m*, it's one of the two languages known as Gaelic. If the accents are acute (´), it's Irish Gaelic; if they are grave (`), it's Scottish Gaelic.

And then there is a language whose identification requires no fewer than three steps. (1) If the text has little hooks, like so: *č*, *š* and *ž*, and (2) the combination *lj* is used frequently, but (3) the letter *đ* is not, then – and only then – it's Slovene.

Which brings us back to the language that so baffled us at the start of this chapter. Where on earth – or where in Europe to be more precise – would the words *Ööbik võib laulda terve öö ehast koiduni* make sense? The *ö* looks Teutonic, but the *õ* reeks of Portuguese. Alternatively, if you suspect the sentence somewhat resembles Finnish, you're close, because that's the bigger sister of our mystery language, the only language on our continent in which *õ* and *ö* can co-occur. It's Estonian. And to clear up the last mystery: *Ööbik võib laulda terve öö ehast koiduni* means 'The nightingale can sing all night from dusk till dawn.' A quote from some EU regulation, I suppose.

⇆ It seems that no Estonian words have made it into English.

💡 Inglane – a woman or man from England. English has a serviceable plural, 'the English', but has had no singular since the time of the Angles. We could do with one for Welsh and Irish, too, though Scot is sorted, and Estonian, too, come to that.

26

The Iberian machine gun

Spanish

A conversation in Spanish is akin to a shoot-out: every word sounds like a bullet, every sentence a burst of gunfire. You might think I'm being disrespectful here, but I say it as someone who knows and loves the language. What's more, it's a description that a Spanish reader would recognise. In an article titled 'Metralletas hablantes' ('Talking submachine guns'), the Madrid newspaper *El Público* stated: 'When we speak Spanish, we fire phonemes from our mouths like bullets from the barrel of an automatic weapon.'

The journalist slightly misrepresented the academic research he was reporting on. What François Pellegrino and his colleagues had actually claimed was that Spaniards produce their *syllables* (not their phonemes) faster than speakers of other languages. The imagery, however, was apt. Pellegrino's team found that Spaniards utter an average of 7.82 syllables per second, as against 6.17 for English speakers and 5.97 for Germans; automatic weapons like Uzis and Kalashnikovs fire about 10 rounds per second.

Why do the Spanish rattle on at such a furious pace? Compared to other languages, and notably English, theirs needs a greater number of syllables for the same utterance. The large majority of Spanish words have two or more syllables, while English is teeming with short words: *pequeño* versus 'small', *puente* versus 'bridge', *fanfarronear* versus 'boast' and so on. Hardly ever does an English word have more syllables than its Spanish equivalent. Now, this comparison is not quite precise, since English often needs several words where Spanish can do with one (*saldré*, for example, covers the entire English phrase 'I will go out'). But on balance, Spanish uses more syllables: almost half as many again as English, according to the above-mentioned research, and around fifteen per cent more than related languages such as French and Italian.

You could be forgiven for thinking that might be why Spaniards seem to be in such a hurry talking: they need to use a lot of syllables to make their point. But this in itself is not a compelling reason to speed up. An alternative route would be simply to take one's time. And this does happen in Spanish – not in Europe, but in America. From the USA in the north to Tierra del Fuego in the far south, Spanish is spoken much more slowly than in Spain. Which is handy for us foreigners. For an easy conversation, I'll take a Peruvian over a Spaniard any day. The difference in speed between the Spanish of the Old and New Worlds is so great that even Latin Americans who move to Spain find themselves facing a language barrier. This is partly caused by the different accent and variations of vocabulary, but initially the murderous speech rate is the biggest obstacle. So the image of 'talking submachine guns' applies only to Spaniards, and thus to a fairly small minority – around ten per cent – of the world's native Spanish speakers.

But what exactly do we mean when we say that Spaniards speak quickly? Is it the case that they deliver an unusually high number of sounds in any given unit of time? Well, no. Spanish syllables are quite short: on average only 2.1 phonemes,

IT'S A LOT EASIER TO UNDERSTAND WRITTEN THAN SPOKEN SPANISH. AT LEAST WHEN IT IS SPOKEN BY SPANIARDS. (CARTOON BY INNUSIK)

compared to 2.7 in English and 2.8 in German. This means that German, English and Spanish speakers alike all pronounce between 16 and 17 phonemes per second – the Spaniards even a fraction less than the other two. Seen in this light, their speech is not quite as fast as first thought. Yet Spanish crucially *sounds* faster than these other languages, and this is largely due to the high number of syllables squeezed into each second. It is syllables, not phonemes, that determine how we experience the speed of a language. If you want to imitate the sound of a gun, you shout something like 'rat-a-tat-tat'. That is, a succession of short, quick syllables. A shout of equally few syllables but many phonemes per second, like 'rarks-rarks-rarks-rarks', doesn't sound like gunfire at all. More like a disturbance in a rookery.

There's another reason why Spanish sounds more percussive than Germanic languages such as English, Dutch and German. Even when the syllables are short and are spoken very quickly – something like 'How do you say "literature" in Russian?', for instance – the Germanic languages still don't come off like an automatic weapon. The reason the Spanish equivalent – *¿Cómo se dice 'literatura' en ruso?* – does have that rattling effect is that all Spanish syllables take the same amount of time. Or more precisely: we experience the syllables as being equally long. If you measure them carefully, it turns out that they are not of identical length. But it is thanks to the seemingly uniform rhythm that the language resembles a submachine gun.

This is not the case for English, German and Dutch. In these languages, the stressed syllables occupy more time than the unstressed. So in passing conversation the sentence 'How do you say "literature" in Russian?' sounds almost like 'How-je say litretcha in Rushn?' Not a staccato rhythm – more a pronounced smack here and there with some mumbling in between.

....

⇆ 'Cork' is a very early borrowing from Spanish – it goes back to 1300. Many more would follow, such as 'armada', 'maize', 'mosquito', 'guitar', 'aficionado', 'potato', 'chocolate' and 'barbecue'.

....

💡 *Tíos* – uncle(s) and aunt(s), as a couple or a group. Likewise, Spanish uses *reyes* for the king and queen together.

27

Mountains of dialects

Slovene

Whether they're from the Baltic port of Kaliningrad or from Vladivostok on the Sea of Japan, there's little difference in the way Russians speak. In Poland, the same holds true: North Poles and South Poles can chat away effortlessly to each other, as can West and East Poles. Even people speaking *different* Slavic languages can often communicate without much trouble. Bulgarians can converse with Macedonians, Czechs with Slovaks, and Russians with Belarusians and Ukrainians. And, for all their political differences, there is no great language barrier between Croats, Bosnians, Serbs and Montenegrins. In fact, as the eminent nineteenth-century Slovak scholar Ján Kollár suggested, the Slavic world could, with no great effort on the part of its citizens, adopt just four standard languages: Russian, Polish, Czechoslovak and, lastly, what you might call Yugoslav or South Slavic.

There is one language, however, that wouldn't so easily be absorbed into Kollár's scheme: Slovene, also known as Slovenian. Admittedly, this is the language of a very small nation. Its entire territory fits no fewer than twelve times into the area of the UK (which is itself not large) and the population, at just over two million, is just a quarter of that of London. And yet, when Slovenes speak their local dialects, many of their compatriots can make neither head nor tail of what they are saying. So just imagine how these dialects would bewilder the members of some of the other nations that Kollár lumped together as 'South Slavic', such as the Bulgarians.

How come? Why does Russian span more than four thousand miles from west to east with next to nothing in the way of dialect diversity, whereas the Slovene language area, measuring just two hundred miles from end to end, is a veritable smorgasbord of regional varieties? Which in turn raises the question: how do dialects come about in the first place?

One school of thought, or rather thoughtlessness, holds that dialects are corrupted forms of the standard language – as, for example, in the view that 'Scouse is just bad English'. This might be one's automatic reaction, but it's in fact the wrong way round: dialects come first, and tend to be at the root of any standard language, which is always an artefact. It would be nearer the truth to claim that standards are 'corrupted', 'unnatural' or 'perverted' dialects. For any other variation of any language, regional or otherwise, develops in a largely unselfconscious way, influenced chiefly by its degree of isolation and contact.

Of these, contact is more obvious but less significant. If people are in frequent communication with speakers (or even writers) of other languages, they will borrow words they find useful, either to express ideas that are more easily expressible in the alien language or to impress their peers. If these people who are in frequent contact with more than one language are children, they may grow up bilingual, which will result in some mutual influence between their languages in terms of vocabulary, grammar and pronunciation. These two types of contact explain why English has loanwords from French, Scandinavian, Latin,

Greek, Dutch, Hindi and many other languages, why its grammar might have been influenced by the grammar of Welsh* and why it is pronounced differently by Pakistanis than by Scots – and differently again by the tens of thousands of Scottish Pakistanis.

Does this explain the variety of Slovene dialects? Yes, to some extent. The Slovene lands – that is, Slovenia and the surrounding areas where the same language is also spoken – may be small, but they adjoin no fewer than four other languages, three of which belong to different language families: Italian to the west (Romance), German to the north (Germanic, of course) and Hungarian to the east (Finno-Ugric). Only Croatian, to the south, is a kindred Slavic language. The Slovene dialects spoken in and near Italy have been influenced by Italian, those spoken in and near Austria by German, and so on. This makes these dialects harder to follow for Slovenes from elsewhere.

But languages are always changing, with or without contact – this is why every generation of adults thinks that young people can no longer talk or write properly. Grandparents and grandchildren, though they communicate smoothly enough, spot many oddities in one another's choice of words, pronunciation and even syntax. This is as true in Slovenia as it is in Britain.

In these days of high mobility, mass media and instant telecommunications, any durable change in British English, for example, ripples through the country from the main urban centres all the way to Cornwall and Shetland. Not so in the past, when people were more likely to spend their whole lives in one or two villages and travel no further than the nearest market town. Talking to an outsider was so rare an event it was unlikely to leave an imprint on anybody's dialect. Language change was very much a local process – spontaneous and haphazard.

---

* In his book *Our Magnificent Bastard Tongue: The Untold History of English*, John McWhorter argues that indeed it has been. For the time being, this is a minority position.

A (LARGELY) PEACEFUL, MOUNTAINOUS COUNTRY IS A GOOD PLACE FOR DIALECTS TO DEVELOP.

Given enough time and isolation, any community's language will become notably different from its neighbour's. The longer the time and the more complete the isolation, the more peculiarities it will accumulate: unique words, a quirky grammar and a pronunciation very much its own. This explains why British English is so much more diverse than American English, in spite of Britain's much smaller size. After all, British dialects spent many more centuries growing apart. And this they continued to do until a turning point was reached around 1900 or so, after which they began slowly to lose some of their distinctiveness.

As in Britain, and perhaps even more so, dialects in Slovenia had plenty of opportunity to develop. The Slovenes settled here in the sixth century and a good part of their new home was mountainous enough to dissuade people living in one valley from visiting the next, let alone travelling any further. For many centuries the small nation belonged to comparatively benign, stable, multi-ethnic empires, such as those of the Carolingians and the Habsburgs. While state and religious affairs as well as urban business activities were conducted in various foreign languages, the Slovene peasants lived their uneventful lives in Slovene, milking their cows, harvesting their crops and gradually changing their dialects. Should any of them have been ambitious or eccentric enough to dream of emulating the national elites' grammar and pronunciation, they would have found this practically impossible, as it was rare for writers or elites to express themselves in Slovene before the mid-nineteenth century.

The other Slavic languages found themselves in very different positions. Russian, Ukrainian, Belarusian and Polish have always been spoken in predominantly flat countries, and their histories are a swirl of conquest, defeat, migration and other events that uproot and mix populations, levelling out their dialects in the process. To a lesser degree, this is also true for Czech and Slovak.

Like Slovenia, some of the Slavic lands to its south – the rest of the former Yugoslavia and Bulgaria – are quite mountainous, which is why dialect diversity is rather more marked there than in the Slavic languages further to the north. In other respects, however, these Southern Slavic areas are different from the Slovene lands. For one thing, a tradition of writing in the vernacular took root earlier and much more firmly. And for another, their political fate was different. Unlike Slovenia, much of the Balkans was steamrollered by the advancing Ottomans, and after centuries of occupation they were the scene of wars of independence. All this turmoil led to more mixing of populations than in Slovenia, which escaped most of the butchery. The more populations are mixed, the less diverse their dialects.

Such mixing has, of course, become commonplace in present-day Slovenia. The country is now an EU member with a modern economy, and people routinely commute over longer distances than their ancestors would have travelled in a lifetime.

Slovene dialects are becoming more and more homogenised, and will probably end up being almost indistinguishable from supermarket milk. In fact, a 'milky' colloquial Slovene is already becoming a second standard language. The first, known as Contemporary Standard Slovene, is in essence the same as the written language, carefully pronounced just as it's spelt, and preserving a number of old traits that no longer exist in many dialects. The emerging second standard, on the other hand, is based on the modern dialect of the capital, Ljubljana. Its detractors deplore its sloppy pronunciation (not all syllables are pronounced and 'tone' or word melody is disregarded) and complain that some of its grammar is wrong (certain endings are no longer used). But today's errors tend to become tomorrow's correct usage, and no one should be surprised if the whole nation were to shift from regional dialects and Contemporary Standard Slovene to the new variety.

Unless, of course, the Slovenian cultural elites manage to maintain Contemporary Standard Slovene among themselves. In that case, they will end up creating a highly unusual phenomenon: a country in which the only dialect is a mark of the upper crust.

⇆ Slovene has given the world one word: *karst*, a geological term for a landscape riddled with sinkholes and water-formed caves. *Karst* reached English through German; the Slovene form was *kras*.

🌱 *Vrtíčkar* – strictly speaking no more than a hobby gardener with an allotment, but the word also suggests that the person is more interested in spending time drinking beer with other *vrtíčkars* than in growing vegetables and flowers. It could be extended in English to refer to people with any hobby that's a cover for conviviality.

28

Hide and speak?

Shelta and Anglo-Romani

Some varieties of English have traditionally been described as cryptolects (or 'secret languages'), because they were developed by groups who wished to communicate amongst themselves while simultaneously excluding the rest of the society in which they were living. The Cant, spoken by criminals from the sixteenth to eighteenth centuries, is a case of a cryptolect, as is Polari, which emerged among gay men in the early twentieth century, when active homosexuality was a criminal offence. Both languages had so many nouns, adjectives and verbs of their own that outsiders couldn't make head nor tail of them, yet the grammar was clearly English.

Today the British Isles are home to at least two English-speaking groups of people who frequently blend a significant number of non-standard words into their speech, to the extent that these blends have names of their own. One of these is Shelta, spoken by Irish Travellers. The other, Anglo-Romani, is spoken by British Roma or English Gypsies. Are we looking at secret languages here?

The answer is not immediately obvious. Shelta in particular is poorly researched and surrounded by many myths and misconceptions. For one thing, its speakers have never called it Shelta. Depending on their dialect, Travellers call it either Gammon or Cant – the latter being unfortunate, given the criminal associations of the earlier, different Cant. When linguists first discovered Shelta in the late nineteenth century, it was hailed as a new Celtic language. Which was odd, because grammatically Shelta and the Celtic languages are worlds apart. The linguists were probably misled by the sounds of Shelta (its phonology), which are indeed similar to Irish Gaelic, though some of its words, too, can be traced to Irish. These Irish-based etymologies were tortuous and far-fetched, but so much the better, the scholars argued – didn't it prove that the Travellers had cunningly altered their words so as to mislead the outside world?

Current thinking is that Irish Travellers, as an ethnic group, at some point in history spoke Irish, then went through a bilingual phase and ended up, much like the rest of Ireland, speaking English as a first language, but retaining some Irish-based vocabulary and adding new words along the way. Since they lived in some isolation from the mainstream of Irish society, it's unsurprising that their language should have developed differently from Irish English. A desire for collective privacy also seems to have entered into it, but this certainly wasn't the whole story. Among the new coinages, for example, were words for 'elephant' and 'squirrel'; why on earth would a 'secret language' include these? What would Travellers have to hide from the outside world concerning wild native rodents and exotic pachyderms?

Our knowledge about Anglo-Romani is more extensive, but at least one misconception about it is widespread. The name might suggest otherwise, but it isn't the English variety of Romani, the originally Indian language (or group of languages) spoken by

IRISH TRAVELLERS IN 1954. THE TRADITIONAL WAGONS HAVE NOW
VIRTUALLY DISAPPEARED, REPLACED BY MODERN CARAVANS.

Roma in most of continental Europe. When the Roma arrived
in Britain, probably in the early sixteenth century, Romani was
indeed their language, but it fell into disuse in the nineteenth
century. Modern English Gypsies, like Irish Travellers, speak
English most of the time, but they have preserved a good number
of Romani words, and it's this blend that's called Anglo-Romani.

Both languages *can* be used to keep outsiders in the dark, and
any speaker will confirm that they *are* occasionally used that way.
But this doesn't make them 'secret languages' in the sense that
exclusion is their primary purpose. When researchers looked
into the actual use of these languages, they discovered that they

fulfilled mostly an internal function: by using Shelta or Romani words, the speaker makes an appeal to the solidarity and shared values between themselves and the listener. Switching to these un-English words makes it easier to talk about things that might otherwise be in some way awkward.

Romani specialist Yaron Matras cites the example of a four-year-old who is asked by her aunt how she got the piece of bread that she's eating. 'I *chored* ('stole') it', the girl replies, having taken it from a table that the family was preparing for guests. In using this Romani – and hence intimate – word, she admits to her misdemeanour while at the same time appealing to her aunt's affection for her. Likewise Alice Binchy, who has conducted research among Irish Travellers, gives the example of two women in a doctor's waiting room full of non-Travellers, with one saying to the other '*Galyune*, the *needjas* are all *sunyin'* at me, I'm *aneishif'*, which means, 'God, the people are all looking at me, I'm embarrassed.' She's not hiding anything reproachable from the outside world, yet uses Shelta in an attempt to secure the sympathy of her fellow Traveller.

None of this is exclusive to Travellers and Roma, of course. Many of us will accuse politicians of outright *lying*, but our children tell *fibs* and our own untruths are mere *white lies*. What criminals do is *stealing*, but when we steal office stationery or fail to declare taxable income, we prefer terms such as *pocketing* and *avoiding*. Modifying one's vocabulary to avoid embarrassment is a universal human behaviour.

Using 'ethnic' words as a means of bonding is widespread too. When two people from, say, York or Aberdeen meet elsewhere, they are likely to use the odd Yorkshire or Scots word, even if on the whole they stick to Standard English. The same is true for any two Brits of Irish, Pakistani or Trinidadian descent. And even the crucial feature of 'secret languages', the element of concealment, is common in other contexts: when abroad, my wife and I often comment in Dutch on (hopefully non-Dutch-speaking) people around us. Does that mean we're using a secret language?

It seems inaccurate, then, to refer to Shelta and Anglo-Romani as secret languages. And yet, both communities have for a long time been on the margins of Irish and British society. Marginalised people all over the world tend to distrust the forces of the establishment, and have many stories to justify that distrust. Shelta and Anglo-Romani may not have originated as secret languages, but it's not hard to understand why their secrecy has come to be prized as an asset.

....

⇆ 'Bloke' may be of Shelta origin. And if 'pal', 'cove', 'chav', 'rum' (meaning 'strange') and 'lush' ('drunkard') are from Romani, as is often suggested, Anglo-Romani would have been the obvious conduit.

....

💡 *Koarig* – female genitalia. English lacks a word that steers a middle course between anatomical (*vulva, vagina*), vulgarity (words spelt with asterisks) and euphemism (*yoni, flower, cooch*). *Koarig* is closest to the last category, but has the street credibility that comes with Shelta.

PART FIVE

Nuts and bolts

Languages and their vocabulary

Words are the smallest particles of language that can stand alone and still have meaning. But meaning is always subject to change (Portuguese) – as, in some parts of the world, are the names of people and places (Latvia). For the speakers of Sorbian, the humble definite article is a bone of contention, while numerals are a tough challenge to the Bretons. And when it comes to nouns, the Italians have a great range of weights and sizes at their disposal, while the Sami are extremely precise when describing their snow.

29

Export/Import

Greek

Where would we be without Ancient Greek? How would we talk about science and culture if we didn't have words such as *dermatology*, *atom*, *alphabet* and *metaphor*? Of course, instead of borrowing these nouns we *could* do what the Icelanders have done and produce home-grown words such as 'skin lore', 'utter kernel', 'bookstaff row' and 'as-it-wereness'. But even insular Icelandic has not been able to wholly resist the Greeks, and now includes words of Greek lineage such as *xenon*, *lýra* and *arkitekt*. It's probably safe to say that the language of Homer, Plato and Sophocles has infiltrated and enriched every one of Europe's languages.

That being the case, you might assume that the language of modern Athens can be traced directly to the language of the ancient city, just as a river can be traced back to its source. But in fact not all words in contemporary Greek are quite as Greek as they appear. They show, or rather conceal, what we might call various degrees of Greekness.

Among the Modern Greek words that have found a home in other European languages (the so-called 'internationalisms'), many are as Greek as Greek can be. They existed in Ancient Greek, were then borrowed by the Romans and later adopted by other European languages. *Prógnōsis*, for instance, has meant 'foreknowledge, prediction' since Classical times (except that Modern Greek has dropped the final s). *Philosophía* was and is 'philosophy', from the Pre-Socratics to the postmodernists. *Dēmokratía* has always been 'democracy'. Words such as these are the tried and true linguistic heirlooms.

However, some other words of Greek stock have undergone a profound change of meaning since they first arose. The Ancient Greek *plásma*, for instance, originally signified a 'thing that is formed', a meaning general enough to encompass 'figure', 'image' or 'forgery' (and later on yet more, such as 'creature' and even 'pretty woman'). It never meant 'plasma' in the modern biological or chemical sense – these concepts wouldn't emerge until the nineteenth and twentieth centuries. Similarly, a *prism*, derived from the Greek *prísma* (literally 'something sawed'), did not acquire its optical meaning until modern times, though Euclid employed it as a geometrical term. And *programme,* including its variety *program*, can be traced to the Greek *prógramma*, which was a 'written public notice or edict'. Nowadays, of course, *program(me)* has a whole slew of meanings ranging from a 'schedule' or 'broadcast' to a 'computer application'. While in many cases conserving the original sense of such words, Modern Greek has also adopted their international meanings – they are 'loan meanings', as linguists say. On the 'scale of Greekness', therefore, these words score lower than *prógnōsis, philosophía, demokratía* and similar cases, whose form and meaning have survived virtually unchanged.

So we've two degrees on the scale of Greekness: the 'heirlooms', which are unaffected by their international success; and the words that have gained new, international meanings, making them just that little bit less authentic. In addition to these, there's a third and very common category: foreign-built compounds. Many of these compounds were created by Western science in the nineteenth century, when scientists drew inspiration from the two Classical languages to coin a plethora of neologisms that are still in use today: *pharmacology*, *empathy*, *ontogenesis*, *android*, *hypodermic*, *idiolect*, *ichthyophobia* and many, many more.

These compounds consist of building blocks that are easily clicked together. If *ichthyophobia* is 'fear of fish' (literally 'fish-fear') and *pharmacology* the 'science of medicines' ('medicine-knowledge'), it doesn't take a genius to work out that *ichthyology* must be the 'science of fish' and *pharmacophobia* the 'fear of medicines'. While the components of these words are of Greek origin, the words themselves are decidedly un-Greek. And yet Modern Greek has embraced them wholeheartedly, as they are both useful and readily understood. In Greece the science of medicines is *pharmakología* and the tool for listening to a patient's internal goings-on is a *stēthoskópio*.* They treat these words as if they were home-grown, and that's perhaps what most people believe them to be. But it's not far-fetched to say that these are loanwords in Greek, albeit ones of Greek origin.

In some cases, the process has led to curious doppelgängers, one having a higher 'degree of Greekness' than the other. The scientific internationalism *phonetic*, for instance, is derived from the Greek word *phōnē* for 'voice, sound' (as in *telephone*, literally 'far-voice') and means 'relating to the sounds of spoken language'. Its Greek counterpart *phōnētikós* has acquired the same scholarly meaning, but this adjective also exists with the home-grown meaning of 'voice' or 'vocal', as in 'vocal cords' (*phōnētikés chordés*). Another case in point is *osteopátheia*, Greek for 'osteopathy'. Based

---

* Modern Greek is transcribed here according to the same system as Ancient Greek. This is not common practice, as the modern language pronounces several letters rather differently, but it better reflects the continuity in the written language.

LESBÍA IS ANOTHER GREEK WORD THAT HAS ACQUIRED ITS MODERN
MEANING BY BORROWING – WHEN THE VICTORIAN BRITISH INTERPRETED
THE POEMS OF SAPPHO OF LESBOS AS EROTIC. THIS PAINTING, SAPPHO
AND ALCAEUS, IS BY SIR LAWRENCE ALMA-TADEMA (WHOSE MOTHER
TONGUE, INCIDENTALLY, WAS FRISIAN).

on its component parts, the word should refer to 'bone-suffering'
or 'a bone disease', which is how Modern Greek uses it. One word
signifies both a condition and a type of treatment.

Are there any degrees of Greekness beyond the three
mentioned so far: the heirlooms, the loan meanings and the
instantly understandable re-imports? Yes, there is a marginal
fourth degree: lower-quality re-imports. *Utopia* is one. Coined
in England by Thomas More, it was recognisably inspired by
the Greek words *ou* 'not' and *topos* 'place'. No Greek would have
formed such a word, but the Greeks have embraced *utopia* (or
rather *outopía*) anyway. It's a bit like the made-in-Japan word
walkman: the compound doesn't feel English, but that hasn't
stopped us from using it.

150

Likewise, when referring to the principal registers of the male voice, the Greeks use the imported terms: *mpásos* (pronounced as 'basos'), *barýtonos* and *tenóros*. This must seem not quite right, because *barýtonos* literally means 'heavy, deep tone' – which would describe the lowest vocal range rather better than *mpásos*, which comes from the Latin word *bassus*, meaning merely 'low'. Another oddity is the *stēthoskópio*. We use 'stethoscope' unthinkingly, but Greeks must sometimes wonder why this clinical instrument is called a chest-*watcher* when it's meant for listening.

Not that the Greeks greatly care about such complications. They're keenly alive to the fact that no living language has influenced Europe's linguistic landscape more profoundly than theirs. No strange foreign coinages or confusing double meanings can in any way dent the pride they feel for their language – or rather, their *hyperēphanía*, to use the (Ancient) Greek word.

....

⇆ Some words borrowed from Ancient Greek are more mundane than the ones discussed above: 'butter' and 'school' are cases in point. Modern Greek adoptions include 'feta' and 'ouzo'.

....

💡 *Krebatomourmoúra* – literally 'bed murmuring', similar in meaning to 'pillow talk', but with a greater element of discord.

30

Arrival in Porto

Portuguese

....

To the Romans, the word *plicare* originally meant 'fold up' or 'roll up'. And to the Catalans, Italians and French who have inherited it (as *plegar, piegare* and *plier,* respectively), it still means 'to fold'. But *plicare* has also travelled east, west and overseas, and along the way it has collected a curious jumble of meanings.

One of them is 'to leave'. This is what the Romanians use it for, in the form *pleca*. This meaning may seem strange, but anyone who has ever been camping will see the logic: folding up your tent is what you do right before you leave. Similarly, when we 'send someone packing', we don't care whether they pack their things; what matters is that they beat it. According to one theory, the shift in meaning from 'folding' to 'leaving' can be attributed to the Roman armies that occupied the area of present-day Romania in the second century. But another, more credible, theory is that the 'folder-uppers' in question were the Romanians themselves, who for many centuries led predominantly nomadic lives. And if anyone knows a thing or two about camping, it's itinerant herders.

LISBON MONUMENT TO THE PORTUGUESE SEAFARERS, MANY OF WHOM
CHEGARAM (ARRIVED) IN INTERESTING PLACES – GIVING RISE TO ITS
NAME, THE MONUMENT OF THE DISCOVERIES.

While the Romanians spent the Middle Ages living as nomadic
landlubbers, on the other side of Europe the Portuguese were
exploring the seas. It is no coincidence that the name of their
country as well as that of their second city, Porto, is derived
from the Latin *portus* ('port'). They also inherited *plicare* from
Latin (and, following their usual practice of converting *pl* at the
start of a word into *ch*, turned it into *chegar*). But as seamen, they
folded and rolled very different things – especially sails. And not
when they were departing – that, of course, was when they had
to unroll and hoist the sails – but rather when they had reached
their destination. As a result, in Portuguese the word developed
exactly the opposite meaning: 'to arrive'.

Incidentally, that the word for 'arrive' stems from shipping is
by no means exceptional. Sailing was for centuries the only way
to travel great distances at speed. The same Catalans, Italians and
French who retained *plicare* for 'fold' have an equally nautical

term for 'arrive': *arribar, arrivare, arriver*. This literally means 'going ashore', from the Latin *ad* ('to') and *ripa* ('shore').

Another language has given *plicare* a meaning that lies precisely in between the Portuguese and the Romanian: English. In English, 'ply' can mean 'fold' or 'layer' (as in 'plywood'), but it can also mean 'to regularly travel over' – as in, 'the ferries ply the route from Newhaven to Dieppe'. In this case, the road travelled by *plicare* is more complicated. In Latin, a verb *applicare* emerged, with the prefix *ad-*, meaning something along the lines of 'to steer a course'. Via Old French *apl(o)ier*, this morphed into the English 'apply'. In the sense 'to travel over' it lost its unstressed initial sound and became simply 'ply'.

All in all, *plicare* has thus covered some complicated (*complicado*) ground. But what does this imply (*implica*)? My reply (*réplica*) to this question would be that it displays the amazing pliability of language. And speaking of displays, whenever you use your smartphone you're engaging with yet another offspring of *plicare* – 'app' is short for 'application' (*aplicação*), a word that's derived from the same Latin verb as eight other English words (and four in Portugese) in this single paragraph.

....

⇆ Most Portuguese loans hail from the colonies, including 'dodo', 'banana' (local words), 'fetish' and 'caste' (Portuguese words for colonial phenomena). One loanword of domestic Portuguese origin is 'baroque'.

....

💡 *Pesamenteiro* or *pesamenteira* – literally a 'condolence-person', used for a funeral-crasher, a quasi-mourner who attends only for the food and drink.

31

Meet the Snorbs

Sorbian

The Sorbs are ashamed of their articles: they think there's no place for irritating little words like *the* or *a* in a proper, self-respecting Slavic language. Not that the rest of the world, Slavic or otherwise, pays much heed. That the mother tongue of some fifty thousand people in the southeast corner of the former GDR is not German, but something akin to Czech and Polish that's called Sorbian, is not exactly common knowledge. To the Sorbs, though, it's a vital question of self-identity.

Hemmed in on all sides by German, the Sorbs would like their language to sound like that of their Slavic brethren. And Czech and Polish simply do not have articles. On the other hand, Czech and Polish frequently use the words 'one' (*jeden*) and 'that' (*ten*). Strictly speaking, these are not articles. 'One' is a numeral and 'that' a demonstrative. But numerals and demonstratives are the types of words that – given enough time – can spawn articles. The English *the* began life as a masculine demonstrative (*that* was its neuter sibling), and the old word for *one* was *an* – pronounced to rhyme with *rain*, but already looking like the

SORBIAN CULTURE AND LANGUAGE WAS REVIVED IN EAST GERMANY
AFTER A PERIOD OF NAZI REPRESSION.

article it would later become. Similarly, the masculine article *un* ('a') in various Romance languages comes from the Latin numeral *unus*, 'one', and the feminine article *la* ('the') comes from the Latin demonstrative *illa* ('that'). Even in this day and age, articles are not always easy to recognise. *Une maison* (French), *una casa* (Italian and Spanish), *ein Haus* (German): all of these could mean 'a house' or 'one house' depending on the context. Likewise, *das Haus* is not only 'the house' but also 'that house' – though for the latter you'd be more likely to say *das Haus da*, 'that house there'. In short: the borders are blurred.

A numeral or a demonstrative doesn't become an article overnight. It takes centuries, during which time the words gradually become more and more *like* articles. In English, French and many other Western European languages, this development is complete. Not so in Czech and Polish: the words 'one' and 'that' are much more common than in Russian (another Slavic language), but less so than articles in English, German or French. In Czech and Polish you can usually omit them without the sentence sounding strange. In languages with true articles, such as English, the articles are obligatory. So 'one' and 'that', in Czech and Polish, have yet to evolve into true articles.

And in Sorbian? It depends. In books translated centuries ago, scribes used *ton* ('that') wherever the German original had a definite article. Back then, it sounded quite normal. And it still does in the modern vernacular. In other words: the Sorbian demonstrative 'that' is well on its way to becoming an article. Moreover, when modern-day Sorbs want to use 'that' as a demonstrative, they often say 'that there' to differentiate it from the more common use of 'that' as an article. But according to the Sorbian establishment, articles in a Slavic language are just not right. As a result, cultured Sorbs (let's call them 'Snorbs') steer clear of articles in their writing. If they mean 'the teacher', they say *ton wučer*, but they write only *wučer*, without the *ton*.

The funny thing is: the Sorbian establishment is mistaken. It is simply not true that Slavic languages have no articles. Granted, it was true in the past. Two thousand years ago almost no European language had articles – only the ancient Greeks, as so often, were ahead of their time. But since then, most languages have developed articles. The Romance languages were the first, with the Germanic languages hot on their heels and a few Slavic languages following slightly later: Bulgarian, Macedonian and – arguably – Sorbian. Seen in this light, Sorbian is a step ahead of Polish, Czech and Russian. Articles are a sign of progress! Articles are modern! It's time the Sorbs put their shame behind them and embraced their articles with pride.

....

⇆ The word 'quark' – for a continental soft cheese – comes from German, which borrowed it from Sorbian. The identical word for a type of subatomic particle was coined by US physicist Murray Gell-Mann, partly inspired by a sentence in James Joyce's *Finnegans Wake*, partly – it has been suggested – by the word for 'cheese', as Gell-Mann's parents were German speakers.

....

💡 *Swjatok* – the enjoyable hours that follow the end of the working day. Equivalent to what the Germans call *Feierabend*, 'evening of celebration'.

32

From our Vašingtona correspondent

Latvian

The French war-time leader Sharrl de Goal was a great admirer of Megell de Therbahntess's famous novel *Don Kihotay*, while the highest-ranking Nazi military leader, Hairmon Gurring, preferred Jovannee Bowcahchow's *Daycahmayron*.

These spellings look like the work of a ten-year-old, and we can forgive a child for struggling with the spelling of Charles de Gaulle, Hermann Göring, Miguel de Cervantes and Giovanni Boccaccio. With non-dyslexic adults, however, we expect better – unless they are guidebook writers, trying to clarify the pronunciation of foreign words and phrases. But in Latvia, this kind of spelling is the official way. Latvians are thoroughly familiar with *Šarls de Golls* and also *Dons Kihots*, written by *Migels de Servantess*. And they've not forgotten *Hermanis Gērings*, nor his favourite book, the *Dekamerons* of *Džovanni Bokačo*.

Looking at a Latvian newspaper, you'd be forgiven for thinking that everyone in the world has a Latvian name. They're all spelt

in Latvian and have Latvian suffixes: most men's names have an
–s added to them, and women get an -e or -a. Even James Jones
becomes *Džeimss Džonss*, with a double *s*, because otherwise he
could be mistaken for the stem *Džeim Džon* (Jame Jone). Place
names get similar treatment: *Maskava, Neapole, Minhene* for
Moscow, Naples, Munich. Of course, many languages translate
the names of famous cities into their own tongue: Moscow,
Naples and Munich are known locally as Moskva, Napoli and
München. But Latvian does this for all sorts of cities: *Kembridža,
Jorka* (and *Ņujorka*), *Oslas, Leipciga, Ēksanprovansa* and so forth.
(Cambridge, York, New York, Oslo, Leipzig, Aix-en-Provence.)
It makes you wonder how obscurer places, such as Auchinlek,
Beaulieu, Tideswell and Ulgham, appear in Latvian papers.
Hopefully never at all.

Latvians are far from alone in this habit of translation.
Lithuania, a neighbouring country with a closely related language,
has the same tendency, albeit less markedly than in the past:
Margareta Tečer is nowadays more likely to be recalled as *Margaret
Thatcher*. But the Latvians have kindred spirits in another corner
of Europe, too: in the Albanian language area, journalists write
about *Margaret Theçer* and *Xhorxh W. Bush*. The Czech Republic
and Slovakia are no strangers to this practice, either. There,
men's names go unchanged, but foreign women find themselves
lumped with the same suffix that Czech and Slovakian women
get: *Margaret Thatcherová, J. K. Rowlingová*. Only the strongest of
international brands – like *Britney Spearsová, Jennifer Lopezová*
and *Céline Dionová* – are sometimes spared the -ová.

The fact is, the rest of Europe used to do the same thing, but
has since grown out of the habit. Take the famous Roman poet
Ovidius. We know him as Ovid, and elsewhere he is variously
called *Ovide, Ovidio, Óivid, Ovidijus, Ovidiu, Ovidi, Ovidije, Owidiusz*
and *Ovīdijs*. Kings' names, too, have long been translated:
Charlemagne is known elsewhere as *Karl den Store, Carlos Magno,*

Carol cel Mare, Kaarle Suuri and so on. And consider the sixteenth-century northern Frenchman Jehan Cauvin. In standard French, this became Jean Calvin. The rest of Europe uses a local variant of his first name (like *John, Ján, Giovanni, Johannes* or *Jehannes*) and often morphs his surname in all sorts of imaginative ways as well: *Calvino, Calví, Calvijn, Cailvín, Kalvyn, Kalwin, Kalvinas* and *Kalvinos*.

As communication between countries and people began to proliferate, this custom started to fade. By the late eighteenth century, names like that of the American president George Washington were indigenised far less often. A German biography translated from English in 1817 referred to him as *Georg Waschington*, but no German would dream of writing that now. In the Romance language areas, one can still stumble across nineteenth-century streets named after *Georges, Jorge* or *Giorgio* Washington. In his day Eastern Europe had much less contact with the West than it does today, so the presidential last name had to be tweaked: *Džordž Vašington* (Croatian), *Jerzy Waszyngton* (Polish). For Albania, this practice continues: the capital boasts not only a *Xhorxh Uashington* street but also a *Xhorxh Bush* street. The Lithuanians have gone one step further with *Džordžas Vašingtonas*, including suffixes. But the Latvians take the cake: the man is called *Džordžs Vašingtons* and the city named in his honour is *Vašingtona*. Clearly, they just can't do without these suffixes.

⇆ English has no loanwords from Latvian.

💡 *Aizvakar* – Latvian is one of many languages that have one word for 'the day before yesterday' (for which English used to have 'ereyesterday'). It's much rarer in also having a word for 'three days ago': *aizaizvakar* (literally: ere-ere-yesterday).

33

Small, sweet, slim, sturdy, sexy, stupid little women

Italian

Donna is the Italian word for 'woman'. This is straightforward enough, but a *donna* is frequently not merely a *donna*. She's often adorned with a tail of extra letters, turning her into a *donnina*, a *donnetta* or a *donnicina*, to name but three of the commonest varieties. And while these suffixes make the word longer, they tend to make the woman in question smaller. On other occasions, though, they make her more attractive, or might even suggest that the speaker – male or female – is not taking her seriously or thinks she's ugly. When an Italian woman is given a garland of extra syllables, she knows all too well they are more than mere decoration.

What the Italians are doing here is not exceptional, but compared to their neighbours they are exceptionally keen on it. Words like *donnina* are called diminutives and are found throughout Europe, except for Scandinavia. In English, however, they are quite scarce, though the –ie suffix is used to create diminutives such as 'Ronnie', 'hottie', 'sweetie' and so on. And English does have a lot of old diminutives, such as *kitten* (a small cat), *darling* (a small dear), *towelette* (a small towel) and *buttock* (a small butt – half the size, to be exact). There is, however, no mechanism for the routine production of new ones. In Italian, on the other hand, there are loads.

This is odd, in a way. Italian obviously has its roots in Latin – the very word *diminutivo* comes straight from Latin – but unlike contemporary Italians, the old Romans had no such wealth of diminutives. Their 'woman', *femina*, had exactly one diminutive, *femella*, which has given us *female*. Another word for 'woman', or rather 'lady, mistress', *domina* (the origin of *donna*) had the diminutive *dominula*. For each noun, Latin had one diminutive rather than a whole suite, as modern Italian does.

This is a bit of a problem for Italian lexicographers. Whereas the writers of Latin dictionaries can just add 'dim.' to an entry and move on, Italian lexicographers have to faff about with all sorts of explanations. For instance, *donnicciuola* denotes a woman of 'lesser spirit', according to the renowned nineteenth-century dictionary Tommaseo-Bellini, while *donnettaccia* expresses disdain. A *donnicciuoluccia*, by contrast, describes a very small woman, and is not intended as an insult per se – though occasionally it may be. These last three words are nowadays somewhat outmoded, but the forms mentioned above – *donnina*, *donnetta* and the like – are all in use, and each has its own nuances. Yet all are simply termed *diminutivi*, a label that fails to do justice to their sheer abundance and complexity.

In addition to all sorts of diminutives (some outdated or regional, several alive and widespread), Italian also has a raft of so-called augmentatives, which are the opposite of diminutives: they denote bigness, or qualities associated with large size. Whereas English augmentatives are formed by means of prefixes such as *super-, mega-, hyper-* and so forth, Italian creates a rather

BELLA! BELLA! BELLISSIMA! ACTRESS GINA LOLLOBRIGIDA IN THE 1960S.

more extensive arsenal of augmentatives by means of suffixes. Thus *donnona*, *donnone* and *donnotta* all signify a woman of some largeness, but they are not quite synonyms: a *donnotta* is biggish and ungraceful, but she's not necessarily mannish, unlike the *donnona*, and she's certainly not as hefty as the *donnone*, who might also be a woman of figurative heft, a 'Signora Big'. Augmentatives are not unique to Italian: they make an appearance in most Romance languages, many Slavic languages and Greek as well. Other languages also have their ways and means of indicating 'bigness', of course; they just don't have an array of special suffixes expressly for that purpose.

In addition to diminutives and augmentatives, Italians also have *dispregiativi* (pejoratives) and *vezzeggiativi* (perhaps best translated as 'affectives'). The tricky thing is that they are often hard to distinguish from diminutives. A *donnetta* could just be small, but the speaker may also intend the word as a term of endearment or of condescension. A *donnuccia* is sometimes just a touch short, but is sometimes a real pain to deal with. It's even possible for *donna-* words to have a plurality of suffixes joined end to end, one indicating a modest size, the other a bad character. Take *donnettaccia*, for example: the *ett* makes her small, the *acci* unpleasant. In other cases, all signs are bad: a *donnacchera*, *donnaccia* or *donnucciaccia* will mean nothing but trouble.

Do all Italian nouns have so many forms? Well, no: for most words, only a limited number of derivatives are in common use. It's enough to make you wonder why the language has a need for so many ways to belittle its women. The usual (and usually the best) explanation for any supposed bias in a language is pure chance. That said, you need only watch an hour or two of prime-time weekend Italian TV to conclude that if this is chance then chance really knows what it's doing.

....

⇆ Many Italian words are instantly recognisable, such as 'spaghetti', 'libretto' and 'portico'. Less conspicuous are 'bank', 'arsenal' (an Italianised Arabic word) and 'manage'.

....

⚲ *Ponte* – literally 'bridge', but also a Monday or Friday taken off so as to connect a public holiday to a weekend.

34

A snowstorm in a teacup

Sami

How many words do the Sami* have for snow?

For a time it was alleged that another famous Arctic people, the Inuit, had dozens or even hundreds of words for snow. This claim was propagated by Benjamin Lee Whorf – a talented if somewhat mystically inclined linguist – in a 1940 issue of the non-academic journal *Technology Review*. He neglected to mention which of the Inuit languages he was talking about (was it Greenlandic, Inuktitut, or something else altogether?), but in any case his assertion was soundly rebutted in 1991 by Geoffrey Pullum, in an article titled 'The Great Eskimo Vocabulary Hoax'. Pullum's investigation debunked a host of supposed Eskimo snow words: as it turned out, *igluksaq* did not mean 'snow for building an igloo' but simply 'building material'; *saumavuq*, likewise, was

---

* The Sami are better known as the *Lapps*, but they'd rather not be called that. Their aversion to the name is not entirely rational, as the name *Lapps* originates from Sami and refers to reindeer husbandry. This seems an apt description, given that they practice this honourable vocation on a large scale. But *Lapps*, apparently, recalls a Swedish word meaning 'rags' or 'tatters'. So Sami it is.

not 'covered in snow', but merely 'covered'. And so on. According to Pullum, 'the *Dictionary of the West Greenlandic Eskimo Language* (1927) gives just two possibly relevant roots: *qanik*, meaning "snow in the air" or "snowflake", and *aput*, meaning "snow on the ground".' In a later article Pullum identified two more terms for snow in this language: *piqsirpoq* ('drifting snow') and *qimuqsuq* ('a snow drift'). To date, nobody has found any others.

So that's that, you might think: people who live in the snow don't have more snow words than anyone else. The Inuit don't, and in all likelihood the Sami don't either, just as the British don't have dozens of words for rain, despite a life-long intimacy with it. Naturally, there are expressions involving rain, such as *driving rain* and the more fanciful *raining cats and dogs*. But substantially different words? The list doesn't extend much beyond *shower*, *drizzle*, *downpour* and *deluge*.

But a book by Erkki Itkonen, published in 1989, would seem to provide a counter-argument to Pullum's refutation. Itkonen's *Inarilappisches Wörterbuch* is a dictionary of the Inari-Sami language. Spoken by just a few hundred people, it appears to include around twenty words for different kinds of snow. This is not to suggest I've actually read it – my curiosity has its limits – but a well-respected linguist by the name of Harald Haarmann has, and he's the one who extracted the list of Sami snow words from Itkonen's dictionary (see opposite).

So what's going on here? Does *kamodah* really refer to a 'hard crust of snow in springtime' or is it just 'crust', regardless of what it's on or what it's made of? Likewise, is *syeyngis* really 'soft snow', or just any kind of goo, whether it be mud or cream cheese? In short: are Itkonen's definitions, as listed by Haarmann, any more accurate than the list that Pullum so roundly demolished?

To clarify the issue it's necessary to consult an expert Finno-Ugrist – a specialist in Finno-Ugric languages, such as Finnish, Estonian, Sami or Hungarian. The great Itkonen was just such an

Inari-Sami's 20 words for 'snow'

ääining – freshly fallen snow on bare ground, making it possible to follow the tracks of wild game

ceeyvi – snow hardened by a strong wind to such a degree that reindeer can't forage for food in it

cuanguj – frozen crust of snow

čearga – thin, hard layer of snow, caused by the wind blowing the top layer of loose snow away and hardening the snow below

čyehi – hard layer of ice directly on the ground, produced by autumnal rain that has frozen solid

kamadoh – hard crust of snow in springtime; if you drive over it with a sleigh, it will crack

kolšša – hard, smooth snowfield

lavkke – snow that has fallen on black ice, and is so smooth that reindeer hooves can't get a grip on it

muovla – very soft snow; skis sink into it

purga – light snowstorm

rine – thick snow on tree branches

seeli – snow that is soft all the way through, from the top layer to the very bottom

senjes – pure snow that has become old, brittle and coarse-grained under a layer of new, hard snow

skälvi – high, hard, steep snow dune

syeyngis – snow that's soft enough for a grazing reindeer to dig through

šleätta – wet, melting snow

šohma – slush on top of the ice

šolkka – tramped down, hard snow

vasme – thin layer of fresh snow

vocca – fresh snow that's so loose it gets blown away in the wind

expert, but he is no longer with us, so for an answer I emailed his eminent student Pekka Sammallahti, in Oulu, northern Finland. On one point, Sammallahti put my mind at ease: the twenty words in question do indeed expressly have to do with snow. But as befits an expert, he then went on to hedge his bets:

What constitutes a snow term? There seems to be a continuum, the core group of terms being those describing the quality of snow. The second group, not quite as central as the first one, would consist of terms describing snow formations, the third would describe snow in motion, the fourth group would contain terms for snow in transition to ice, the fifth to water and the sixth to different kinds of areas covered with snow.

Ah! But if this is the case, then we, too, have a whole raft of words for rain. After all, a *puddle*, a *drop* and perhaps even *mist* and *spray* could be called 'rain formations'. A *splash* and a *flood* would be 'rain water in motion', *sleet* the 'transition from rain to snow' and *slush* the 'transition from snow to water'. And *pond*, *creek*, *canal*, *lake* and *lagoon* are all words for 'surfaces covered with rain'.

The conclusion may have to be that there are many similarities between the sets of words that English and Inari-Sami have to describe objects and phenomena that their speakers frequently encounter. (And perhaps this is also true for the Inuit languages – but one contradicts Pullum at one's peril.) The difference is that for English speakers many of these objects and phenomena are chilly, wet and transparent, whereas for the Sami they tend to be frozen solid, white and opaque.

⇆ The Sami group of languages has given the world one word: 'tundra'. Russian has acted as an intermediary for its diffusion.

💡 It is possibly over-ambitious to import all twenty Sami words for snow, but skiers would certainly benefit.

35

Deciphering the language of numbers

Breton

In Breton, the Celtic language of Brittany, counting is easy. Calculating, however, is next to impossible.

To count, you don't need numbers, just counting words, better known as numerals: you start with 'one' and move on to 'two', and so on and so forth until you reach the uncountable. All European languages have a word for 'hundred' and 'thousand', which they can go a long way with. For 'zero', pre-scientific languages simply used 'none' or 'nothing', and the word 'million' is likewise fairly young – literally meaning 'a big thousand', it was formed by talking the Italian word for a thousand, *mille*, and adding the suffix *–one*, meaning 'big'. At the end of the thirteenth century Marco Polo's travelogue was given the title *Il Milione*, probably in reference to what was taken to be his habit of exaggerating. Some time after, the word acquired the more precise meaning of one thousand multiplied by one thousand; later, another numeral was deemed necessary for an even vaster number, and a billion

MENHIRS IN BRITTANY. THEIR NUMBERS ARE BEST CALCULATED IN
FRENCH RATHER THAN BRETON.

was born. Then came a trillion and a variety of numerals used
only in scientific circles, reaching further and further towards
the great uncountable: infinity.

Anyway, that long list of numerals – they're just written-out
numbers, right? Isn't three simply 3 and nine simply 9? And isn't
the logical system of numbers, working its way from right to
left in ones, tens, hundreds and so on, also exactly the same for
numerals? After all, you can clearly identify the numbers 7 and
8 in 'seventy-eight'. It's true that in English 'eleven' and 'twelve'
are exceptions and thirteen to nineteen are back to front, but
for the most part the numerals do correspond to the numbers.

In quite a number of languages, however, this is not the case, and the numerals sound very different to what you might expect from seeing their counterparts in digits.

Take French, for example, with its infamous 'four-twenty-ten-eight' (*quatre-vingt-dix-huit*) for 98. Or Danish, with its baffling 'eight-and-half-fifth' (otteoghalvfems), which we need to interpret as 'eight and half the fifth twenty' in order to get 98, like this: $8 + ((5 - \frac{1}{2}) \times 20)$. And this isn't even the odd one out in the array of Danish numerals – they're all equally odd.

But of all the European languages in which numbers and numerals are out of synch, Breton has to be the hardest. To start with, the system is vigesimal, or based on sets of twenty: 45 is not 'forty-five', but 'five-and-two-twenty'; similarly, 77 is 'seventeen-and-three-twenty'. This is not to say it's consistent: 35, for example, is simply 'five-and-thirty'. And 50 is 'half-hundred'.

It's hard enough to calculate seventy-seven plus fifty-nine in English in your head, but at least our numerals help us visualise our numbers. Imagine doing the same in Breton: seventeen-and-three-twenty plus nine-and-half-hundred. And that's not even a particularly distressing example. If you really want to torment a Breton, ask them to calculate seventy-eight plus fifty-nine. In Breton, the first numeral is three-six-and-three-twenty. So what you're asking them to do is calculate $(3 \times 6 + 3 \times 20) + (9 + \frac{1}{2} \times 100)$: in their head and with no help at all from numerals such as 'eighteen' and 'sixty', because these don't exist in their language. This is why it's easy to count in Breton, but rather more difficult to calculate.

There's an interesting comparison to be made with the Bretons' Celtic cousins, the Welsh. The traditional Welsh counting system has a strangeness all its own: 77 is 'two-on-fifteen-and-three-twenty', 78 is 'two-nine-and-three-twenty' and 79 is 'four-twenty-minus-one'. But at some point they made the wise decision to employ these numerals exclusively for the purpose for which they were intended: denoting numbers. When calculation is involved, the words are different. If a Welsh speaker were asked to add 77 to 79, they would pronounce the numbers as (the Welsh equivalents of) 'seven-ten-seven' $(7 \times 10 + 7)$ and 'seven-ten-nine' $(7 \times 10 + 9)$. It's the most logical method you could imagine – even more logical than Wales's second language, English. Sound advice, I'd say. But will the Bretons heed it? I wouldn't count on it.

⇆ 'Bijou' and 'menhir' have reached English via French, which borrowed them from Breton.

💡 *Startijenn* – a kick of energy, such as you get from a shot of coffee. Probably derived from English *start*.

PART SIX

Talking by
the book

Languages and their grammar

Most languages are saddled with a lot of grammatical stuff that English is spared. Nearly all have genders, which can lead to confusion (Dutch), and many have a case system (Romani). Some endlessly decline their verbs (Bulgarian), while a few suffer from afflictions such as mutation (Welsh) and ergativity (Basque). But there's one language we might think of emulating – Ukrainian, which has an enviable grammatical trick up its sleeve.

36

Gender bending

Dutch

Consider this bit of dialogue: 'Ze heeft mooie poten.' - 'Ja, heeft-ie.' Translated from the Dutch, this could be rendered as: 'She has nice legs.' - 'Yeah, doesn't he.'

This sounds like a case of communication that's gone seriously awry. But if the first speaker is from Belgium and the second from Holland, their conversation may come out exactly this way - provided the admired legs are not a person's but those of, say, a table.

This is possible because Dutch is one of many languages that makes it sound 'as if things had grown genitals', as I once heard an American put it. In other words, every noun has a gender, even a cup of coffee. In fact, a cup of coffee in Dutch has several genders: a *kop koffie* is masculine, a little *kopje koffie* is neuter and a - mostly Belgian - *tas koffie* is feminine. A *tafel* ('table') is feminine in Belgium, but mostly masculine in the Netherlands - hence the mix-up in our little dialogue. A *model*, on the other hand, is always neuter in Dutch, whether the word refers to a Jaguar XJ, Naomi Campbell or David Gandy.

DUTCH MODEL DOUTZEN KROES. IN HER MOTHER TONGUE, SHE'S
CONSIDERED NOT FEMININE BUT NEUTER.

So what does it actually *mean* for a Dutch noun to have a
gender? The answer is: nothing. Gender in this context is just a
grammatical phenomenon that, roughly speaking, determines
two things: the choice of the definite article and the choice of
the pronoun. Whereas all English nouns happily share the single
article 'the', their Dutch counterparts are divided between *de*
(masculine and feminine) and *het* (neuter): *de kop, de tas, de tafel,
het kopje, het model*. Old English, back in the days when years

were three-digit affairs, similarly had gendered nouns, but to speakers of modern English the whole area of gender is a source of aggravation when trying to learn Dutch – or French or German or any of a host of other European languages.

As for pronouns, the English 'it' can refer to pretty much anything that's singular and doesn't breathe. There are some exceptions, as in 'fill her up' and 'Britain calls upon her sons', but they're just that: exceptions. Not so in Dutch: Dutch pronouns are expected to reflect the gender of the nouns they refer to, so that the same cup of coffee can become a 'he', a 'she' or an 'it' (*hij, zij* or *het*) depending on the exact noun the speaker happens to have chosen (*kop, tas, kopje*).

But if the speakers of Old English used to religiously observe this system, and the Germans of today still do, when it comes to pronouns no such grammatical rule of law obtains among the speakers of Dutch. Gender anarchy seems to have become the norm in the Netherlands – though much of what follows does not hold for Belgium and its neighbouring Dutch regions.

If you point out this state of affairs to a group of Dutch people, they will probably say that they are using the old system, albeit with some slight modifications. They might concede that they refer to male and female models as 'he' and 'she' rather than 'it'. And the more language-conscious among them may even agree that many feminine words have 'turned masculine', such as *tafel* and *school*. But anarchy? No way!

Well, they'd be right, to an extent – it's not quite anarchy. But the fact is, the Dutch have thoroughly subverted the old rules, especially in speaking, but have been so blinded by what they learnt back in their schooldays that it took a linguist of foreign extraction – Jenny Audring, a contributor to this book – to figure out just what's been going on. The Dutch language, she has revealed, has undergone nothing short of a gender transformation.

So here's the situation. The use of the word 'she' has become limited to one small category: living beings of whose female sex the speaker is strongly aware. This includes all women, as well as female animals of one's acquaintance, such as pets and horses or, if you happen to be a farmer, sheep, cows and sows. Not all that different from English, really.

But unlike what you would expect as an English speaker, the non-living world has not been colonised by the word 'it'. This feat has been accomplished, to some degree, by its competitor 'he'. Regardless of their traditional gender, all singular objects are now referred to as 'he': a cup of coffee, an aeroplane, an atom, a planet, you name it. Men and all other living beings that are not manifestly female are also lumped in this object category – a blatant act of linguistic sexism. As for the third and last singular pronoun – 'it' has been assigned to so-called 'mass nouns' such as wine, luggage and information, and to abstract concepts such as joy, honesty and, again, information.

Of course, in every language there's a degree of discrepancy between what's spoken on the streets and what's enshrined in the dictionaries and grammar books. Languages are in a state of perpetual flux, and the so-called rules are necessarily out of synch with the actuality. Old-school English grammarians will tell you, for example, that 'they' is a third person plural pronoun, and must always be used as such. In speech, however, people have for a long time been using 'they' as a singular pronoun in order to avoid specifying a gender, as in 'Any English speaker will tell you that they have used "they" in this way', rather than 'Any English speaker will tell you that he has used "they" in this way'. In time, this usage will become officially acceptable.

That said, Dutch writers do find themselves in a real quandary, because every time they use 'he', 'she' or 'it' they have to think twice. As a linguist I'm thrilled by Jenny Audring's analysis of the way my language is changing right under my nose. As a writer,

178

however, I'm not so happy, because now I know that there are two different sets of rules for Dutch – those of the street, and those of the dictionary – and each time I sit down at my desk I'm forced to choose between them. A fine old mess.

....

⇆ The Low Countries have exported an amazing number of words to the English language: well over 300, from 'beleaguer', 'cruise' and 'coleslaw' to 'plug', 'easel' and 'smuggler'.

....

💡 *Uitwaaien* – relax by visiting a windy place, often chilly and rainy. Since the British, like the Dutch, display this peculiar behaviour, the word would be useful.

37

A case history

Romani

For many English speakers, one particular aspect of learning another European language is a real ordeal: cases. But there's good news: those nasty little buggers are on their way out. The pace of their disappearance is variable, but as surely as water flows downstream, it's happening, in the Indo-European family at least.

Let's look at some examples. For 'wolf ', Latin had the inflectional forms *lupus* and *lupi* and *lupo* and so on; but French, its direct descendant, only has *le loup* left. Old Germanic had *wulfaz*, *wulfasa*, *wulfan* and so forth – six forms in total – but modern German retains just four of the six, and in speech many people use at most three (*der Wolf*, *dem Wolf* and *den Wolf* – notice how the case ending has moved from the noun to its article) and some dialects use only two. In writing there's also the option of *des Wolfes* ('the wolf's'), but anybody using this case – the only real survivor in English – in speech sounds like a voice from the grave.

Cases are few and far between to the north, west and south of the German language area. Only a handful of small languages in the bleak northwest of Europe have preserved them: Icelandic,

ROMA GUITARIST JEAN 'DJANGO' REINHARDT. DJANGO MEANS 'I AWAKE' IN ROMA.

Faroese, Scottish Gaelic and Irish Gaelic – and in Ireland they are languishing. East of the German-speaking world, however, cases are still widespread. Only Bulgarian and Macedonian have managed to shake them off (almost) entirely. The other Slavic languages, plus Albanian, Armenian, Latvian and Lithuanian, all have six to seven cases, while Romanian and Greek are clinging to their last three or four.

Yet in the east, too, there are signs that the system is beginning to crumble. To start with, all the languages mentioned above have fewer cases than the eight proudly boasted by their Proto-Indo-European ancestor five thousand years ago. In various languages the vocative (a form of address like the Latin *amice* – a bit like 'Hey man!') is on its way out. And it is becoming increasingly difficult to recognise certain cases. In Czech, for example, a single word form often has to bear the weight of a large number of cases: *nádraží* ('station'), for example, stands for six inflectional forms in the singular and four in the plural. This is not exactly an aid to clarity. Admittedly, in Central and Eastern Europe cases are far from dead, but the current is flowing in one direction and one direction only: from the case-happy mountain top to the case-free waters downstream. My prediction: in perhaps twenty generations – thirty at most – all these languages will have reached the sea of caselessness.

Or is this prediction too bold? There is one European language that casts doubt on the matter: Romani, the language spoken by millions of Roma. Around the start of the first century AD, when its speakers lived not in Europe, but in India, it still had seven cases. In the following centuries this figure fell to three, in line with our 'water law'. But by the time the Roma began their trek westwards, in the eleventh century or thereabouts, it had risen again, to as many as eight. And modern Romani, broadly speaking, has retained these eight cases.

How can that be? Cases, however irritating they are for English speakers, are not just a nuisance. They provide a service no language can do without: they specify the role of a word in a sentence. If a word is in the nominative case, for example (*lupus, der Wolf*), then it is the subject; in the accusative case (*lupum, den Wolf*) it is the direct object. Some languages have a special case to indicate a place (locative) and yet another to indicate a tool (instrumental). Of course, there are other ways to do this: English, for example, uses a fixed word order and prepositions. In 'Kim gives Lesley money', who is giving what to whom is unmistakeable. Likewise, in 'The girl played with her ball in the garden', it is clear what is being played with and where, despite the fact that there is no case to be found.

But to get back to Romani. When it cast off four of its seven cases, it retained the two that identified the subject and the direct object (plus a third, but that's another story). Most of the other cases were replaced by words like *about* and *by* and *in* – that is, prepositions. Or, more precisely, postpositions, because they appeared after the word they referred to. As do some English 'prepositions': consider the position of 'ago' in the sentence 'Many centuries ago, the language had three cases.'

Eventually – and this is the crux of the matter – these postpositions in Romani attached themselves to the noun. Rather than being words in their own right, they became fixed endings for nouns (that is, suffixes). It is obvious which of these Romani suffixes are old and which are new: the three old cases are short – *phral, phrala, phrales* ('brother') – while the new ones are long – *phraleske, phraleste, phralestar, phralesa* and *phraleskero*. Of course, as an outsider you can't hear whether something is a suffix or a separate word, because spaces are not pronounced. But thanks to all sorts of grammatical signals, native speakers can sense whether something is a separate word or a suffix. No native English speaker would mistake the 'ago' in 'archipelago' for a separate word, or take 'weeks ago' to be a single word.

Rivers never flow upstream. But languages, apparently, can make new cases. Just as water can head skywards again: it evaporates into clouds, travels on the wind and falls as rain, flowing down and then up and down, over and over again, in an eternal cycle. In Romani, too, the cycle continues: in some dialects, the 'new' cases have already disappeared.

....

⇆ 'Pal' is probably of Romani origin, through Anglo-Romani. 'Cove', 'chav', 'rum' (the adjective, not the drink) and 'lush' (for 'drunkard') may have the same roots.

....

💡 *Wortacha* – partner in an economic endeavour. Avoids the ambiguity of the English 'partner'.

38

A much-needed merger

Bulgarian-Slovak

For most outsiders, the Slavic languages – Russian, Polish, Slovak, Bulgarian and the rest – all have the same snag: they're too damned difficult. Not for toddlers, of course, because they can do everything. But for full-grown Germanic speakers like you or me, there's not much hope.

This is not because the Slavs have different names for things. We have no problem learning that a 'hand' is a *ruka* and 'to pay' is *platit*. And nor is it the Cyrillic script that makes the Slavic languages difficult. Cyrillic is not all that complicated, and it's only used by half the Slavic family anyway. No, the problem with the Slavic languages is the grammar. They suffer from the same defect from which Latin suffered: every verb and every noun insists on having a whole array of suffixes. If you learnt any Latin at school, you'll remember how irksome all those declensions and conjugations could be.

The Slavs themselves also know perfectly well that life need not be so hard. Several Slavic languages have come up with partial solutions to the problem of suffix proliferation. The only thing is, they haven't opted for the same approach. The Slavic world is long on good ideas but short on internal communication.

In the interests of opening up the Slavic languages to the multitudes of non-Slavs, I'll try to hurry things along. Here, under my interim management, we shall start the merger of two languages: Bulgarian and Slovak. The choice of languages is somewhat arbitrary, I'll grant you, but not altogether. Both are further down the road of simplification than, say, Belarusian or Serbo-Croatian. We shall call the result of this merger *Slogarian.* A 'best of both' language, it will incorporate two outstandingly helpful properties from each of the merging partners, thus making it The Ideal Slavic Language. The others – Ukrainian, Slovene, et cetera – can follow its example.

ACTION POINT 1 *THE CASES*

Here Slogarian will take over almost an entire Bulgarian department. In Slovak and almost all the other Slavic languages, every noun gets six or seven different case endings in the singular, and another six or seven in the plural. Now, even if these twelve or fourteen suffixes were the same for every word, that would be more than enough. But instead they show ludicrous variation: feminine, masculine and neutral words all get different suffixes, words ending in one letter get different suffixes than those ending in another letter, animate nouns (i.e. words for living things) get different suffixes than inanimate nouns, and then there are words that follow no discernible pattern whatsoever.

Bulgarian, in contrast, wrested itself from this chaos centuries ago. Only its form of address (the vocative) recalls those dark times. On the other hand, Slovak, while generally as case-happy as any other Slavic language, has scrapped the vocative. So there is no reason for Slogarian to retain the vocative either. There we are – no cases left!

ACTION POINT 2 *THE ARTICLE*

Slovak and most other Slavic languages have no article. This is not a huge catastrophe, but as a Germanic speaker you'll be used to using articles: you'll feel like something is missing if you always have to make do without the 'the'. Slogarian, therefore, will retain the articles used in Bulgarian. These come after the noun, so that's something we'll have to get used to. But the Scandinavian languages have that too, so it's not altogether un-Germanic.

ACTION POINT 3 *THE STRESS*

In Bulgarian and quite a few other Slavic languages, the stress is irregular; just as in English, but even worse. In a word like *mezhet* ('the man'), for example, the stress goes at the end. That is to say: on the article! That's like saying '*the* man' instead of just 'the *man*'. What's more, the word *velna* can mean 'wave' or 'wool', depending on the stress. This just won't do. Surely things don't need to be so hard? Happily, they don't, and Slovak provides the proof: the main rule there is simply to emphasise the first syllable. There is also a sub-rule that applies to prepositions, and that's easy to learn as well. Right then – Slogarian will follow this example.

ACTION POINT 4 *THE VERB*

Here Slogarian has no choice but to ignore Bulgarian and embrace the Slovak rules. Slovak (like most of the other Slavic languages) keeps a tight leash on its complexity. It distinguishes between a past tense, a present tense and a future tense, and that's pretty much it. This stands in stark contrast to Bulgarian. A Bulgarian conjugation table looks like a medical encyclopedia: imperfectum, imperfective, futurum secundum exactum, aorist, conditional, inferential, renarrative, dubitative, indicative, passive, and so on and so forth. The renarrative is what you use when the speaker is saying 'I got this from hearsay', the inferential means 'I've inferred this from other information' and the dubitative expresses scepticism – 'I'm saying this, but I'll eat my hat if it's true'. We can, of course, express all these nuances in countless ways in English, but in Bulgarian all these tenses and moods and aspects and voices have separate suffixes for the first, second and third person in the singular and plural, and sometimes also for masculine, feminine and neutral. This seems an unduly complicated solution. Let's not saddle Slogarian with such intricacies.

Two questions remain. One: should Slogarian use the Cyrillic or Latin alphabet? And two: which vocabulary should Slogarian employ? Well, as a Westerner, I'd naturally be in favour of the Latin script. And I'd suggest the Russian vocabulary, because it has lots of Western European words, including English ones like *biznesmen* and *menedjer*. But really, the alphabet and the vocabulary are not the problem. It's the grammar – and I've sorted that out now. All in a day's work.

⇆ English has no loanwords from Bulgarian, with the debatable exception of the name of the Bulgarian currency, the *lev*, which literally means 'lion'.

💡 *Malcha* – Bulgarian for to be silent, to say nothing. An obvious gap in the English vocabulary; most European languages have a simple word for this concept.

39

Nghwm starts with a *C*

Welsh

Although there are exhaustive dictionaries of Welsh, they're not of much use to anyone learning the language.

Take the verb *bod*. One of its forms is *bôm*, which is not altogether bizarre. But its other forms include *basai* and *byddwch*, and then there are *dydyn, dwyt, doeddet, fasen, fyddan, mae, oeddwn, roeddech, rwyt, rydych, wyt* and *ydw*, all of which you'd fail to find in a dictionary unless you knew to look under *bod*. But, of course, if you already knew that they are variations of the verb *bod*, you wouldn't need to look them up in a dictionary, would you?

Now, *bod* is the Welsh verb for 'to be', and the verb 'to be' is regularly irregular in the languages of Europe – 'am', 'is', 'were' and 'been' also look nothing alike. What's more, a number of the Welsh forms above seem more capricious than they really are. There is a certain logic to them, albeit one that escapes outsiders. This, again, is not exactly exceptional. Would an outsider think to look up the English word *ate* under e, for instance?

Yet none of this changes the fact that the repertoire of Welsh word forms is astonishingly ornate. Suppose you read the word *nghymoedd.* You will search in vain in the dictionary. Naturally, because it's a plural, and plurals don't have separate entries in the dictionary. The last letters, *-oedd*, are a fairly common plural marker in Welsh, but in this case the plural form is created not only by adding a suffix to the singular form – the vowel, too, is different. In the singular, the vowel is not *y*, but *w*, pronounced as *oo*. Crazy, right? Oh wait – the vowel change happens with 'man'/'men' too; and then there's 'goose'/'geese'.

Right: putting the suffix *-oedd* aside, and replacing the *y* with *w*, we get *nghwm*. But that seems not to be in the dictionary either. Why not? Because the right place to look for *nghwm* is under *cwm* ('combe', 'valley') – a word that shares just one letter with *nghymoedd*. *Nghwm* and *cwm* are different versions of the same word, and *nghymoedd* is the plural of both. Bear with me, all will soon be clear. And keep in mind, too, that Welsh is by no means the patent holder on strange plural forms. For instance, Russians say *ushi* instead of *ukha*, which is what you would expect the plural of *ukho* ('ear') to be. Likewise, the French have *yeux* instead of adding an *s* to *œil* ('eye') to make the plural, and let's not forget English, with its *mice* for *mouses*. And once upon a time, the plural of *cow* was *kine* – words that share not a single letter.

What is typically Welsh, though – or rather typically Celtic – are the changing consonants at the beginning of words. There is a system to this: nouns and adjectives whose initial consonants change are following fixed rules. Those starting with a *c* all behave just like *cwm*, those with a *p* all do the same as *pont* ('bridge'), and so forth. But it's not an easy system. *Cwm* in the singular has three 'mutations' (the technical term): the soft form *gwm*, the nasal form *nghwm* and the aspirated form *chwm*. *Pont* also has three: *bont, mhont* and *phont*. Some other words have only two mutations, still others only one and some have none. It all depends on the initial sound.

Now, you might expect – at least I did – that each of these different forms has one distinct function. If only it were that simple. The soft form, for example, is used in feminine words when it is preceded by the definite article *y* ('the'). *Pont* is feminine, so 'the bridge' is *y bont*. But *cwm* is masculine, so 'the valley' is *y cwm* – just the basic form, not the soft (as in *Pobol y Cwm*, the Welsh soap opera that has been on air since 1974). If a noun is preceded by the numeral 'one', again only feminine words take the soft form, but after 'two' both masculine and feminine words do. After *dy* ('your') the soft form is used, after *fy* ('my') the nasal form and after *ei* the aspirated form if *ei* means 'her', but the soft form if it means 'his'. (I just looked this up. I wrote it down. And to be honest, it's escaped me already. All that remains is befuddlement.) Thus the arbitrary rules thread themselves together, one after the other. And we haven't even started on the verbs, which also have their own mass of disorderly order, giving rise to all those forms of *bod* that started this chapter.

So why does it all have to be so hard? Paradoxically, the answer is a combination of efficiency, efficiency and some more efficiency, though the end product is a tortuous set of rules.

The first type of efficiency occurs when speakers change some of their language's sounds so as to make them easier to pronounce. This happens all the time, in all languages. In English, for instance, most participles were at one stage pronounced with a 'd', which is why we still spell them with a *d*. In current pronunciation, however, many of these *d*'s are 'sharpened' (or devoiced, to use the technical term) into *t*'s, under the influence of the preceding sharp (or voiceless) sound: *faced* now rhymes with *waste*. Conversely, a *t* may be pronounced as 'd' in some positions. This is atypical of British English but the norm in the American and Australian varieties, making dozens of word pairs, such as *metal* and *medal*, sound identical.

HOW ABOUT SOME BYRGYRS, CEBABAU OR PITSAS? NOT EVERYTHING IS
HARD ABOUT WELSH.

The latter sound change also occurred in Welsh at a very early
stage: the word *catena*, a Latin loan meaning 'chain', morphed
into *cadwyn*, with a *d*. The Celts of old did this even across word
boundaries: in *tabarna teka* ('fair tavern'), the sharp *t* of *teka*
became a soft *d* under the influence of the neighbouring vowels.
(Vowels are great softeners of consonants – it explains how *metal*
can sound like *medal* in the US and Australia and why Welsh turned
the *t* of *catena* into a *d*.) Naturally, this did not happen when a
word like *teka* appeared after, say, *eskopos* ('bishop'), for after the
final sharp or voiceless *s* sound an equally voiceless *t* is perfectly
easy to pronounce: *eskopos tekos* (the *-os* ending replacing the *-a*
is grammatically determined, much like in Latin). This is just an
example, mind you: changes like this also affected a good number
of other consonants, as *cwm* and *pont* have already testified.

At this stage, efficiency measure number two moved in to
wreak a new round of havoc: the dropping of unstressed word
endings. This, again, is not exactly unheard of – both English and

191

French did exactly the same. The word *good*, to name just one example out of many thousands, used to have some ten forms, including *gode*, *godne* and *godum*, before being cut back to the bare essentials. (A good thing, I'm sure you'll agree.) And when Latin evolved into French, the old word *bonus* (also meaning 'good') evolved into *bon* – which, again, was typical of what French did to endings. Needless to say, these changes simplified English and French a good deal, so the efficiency gains were considerable. And as in English and French, so in Welsh: *tabarna* and *teka* shed their final *a*'s and became *tafarn* and *teg*. Now you might expect that since *tafarn* ends in a consonant, 'fair tavern' would from now on simply be *tafarn teg*. But after centuries of pronouncing *teka* with a 'd' because of the preceding 'a', the Welsh had grown attached to it, so that 'fair tavern' became *tafarn deg*. The *d*, having arrived at high tide, was left stranded when the tide went out. In other cases, however, where the noun had not previously ended in a vowel (such as *eskopos*), the Welsh were not inclined to pronounce the *t* as 'd'. Now that words were shorn of their endings, the *eskopos teka* became *esgob teg*: lots of changes, but the old *t* stayed put. And again, this is just an example: all sorts of mutations were stranded in lots of different places.

Time for efficiency measure number three to finish the job, by making the mutation rules more 'logical'. Again, this is something that all natural languages do – recall how English did away with nearly all 'illogical' plurals (*eyen, namen, kine*), retaining only a few oddballs such as *men* and *sheep*. Under the old, complex rules of Welsh, verbs used to cause mutation in some nouns, but not in others. Nowadays, the direct object of a sentence typically undergoes mutation, whereas the subject usually doesn't. This is definitely easier, but there is a downside: mutation no longer serves the ease of pronunciation. And of course many nouns do not undergo mutation at all, because it depends on the first letter (remember?) and often on the gender, too.

Big deal, you may say. As long as people can speak their language, surely there's no need for them to understand why the grammar is as it is or how it came to be that way? Fair point, but it does mean that its succession of efficiency measures has landed Welsh with a system that makes life hell for second-language learners, while being riddled with rules that can seem to be all but pointless.

A word which, if it were Welsh, might present itself as *phointless*, *bointless* or *mhointless*. Ah, do spare a thought for Welsh lexicographers. Mhoor tevils.

....

⇆ The Welsh origin of 'penguin', originally a name for the great auk, is controversial. 'Coomb' and 'corgi' are certainly Welsh borrowings, and 'flannel' may be.

....

💡 *Cwtch* – the cupboard under the stairs. Remarkably, the word also means 'hug'.

40

Strictly ergative

Basque

Water flows; mountains do not. Mountains are eroded by the water that streams down their flanks – but they never move. The Indo-European languages are like water. In the course of several thousand years they poured across almost all of Europe (and South Asia), and in some places drained away again. In the last few centuries they have engulfed most of the globe, and now half the world speaks an Indo-European language: English, Spanish, Portuguese, French, the list goes on.

Basque, in contrast, is like a mountain. No matter which language splashed against it – Celtic, Latin, Gothic, Berber – it has remained unmoved for thousands of years. Once upon a time it was probably surrounded by related languages, but these family members have all long since perished. Now Basque is an island language – an isolate, as linguists call it: a mountain rising above the waters, standing all alone in a sea of Indo-European.

Mountains and water – they're both made of molecules, themselves composed of atoms, but other than that they are not alike. Similarly, Basque and Indo-European are both made of words that are made of phonemes, but they are worlds apart in every other way. One of the most peculiar Basque characteristics is known as *ergativity*. Picture this: I'm hesitating, but after a while I decide to pick up the phone and call Jenny. In short: *I hesitate. I call her*. If you want to express the same thing in Basque, you get two sentences that look more like: *I hesitate. Me calls she*. How can this be? Well, to a Basque, these two sentences belong to two completely different categories, each with its own set of rules. The difference lies in the verbs. Hesitating is something that only one person does – the hesitator – but you need two people for calling: the caller and the callee.

In a sentence with only one actor there is no doubt about who is performing the action expressed by the verb. In *I hesitate*, 'I' and 'the hesitator' must be one and the same – both in English and in Basque. In terms of English grammar 'I' is, obviously, the subject. But for reasons that will become clear later on, the term 'subject' is inappropriate in Basque. So let's use the term *Form 1* instead.

The minute another actor comes into play, the situation becomes less clear. We have three components to our sentence: two people plus the call that is being made. But who does what? Who is dialling the number and who hears the phone ringing? As an English speaker, you probably can't see the difficulty here: the caller is the subject, which we have just rechristened *Form 1*, and the callee is the object (let's call her *Form 2*). So it's straightforward: 'I call her'. Where's the problem?

In English there is no problem; in Basque, however, there is. In a sentence where there are two roles, one acting on the other, *Form 1* is not used for the active role (the subject, the agent, the doer, call it what you like), but for the one being acted upon (the object, the patient, the victim). Thus 'Me calls she' is the way to express in Basque what we, in English, would express as 'I call her'.

It is important to get the terminology right. Because in Basque the equivalents of *Form 1* can be used as the subject only of sentences in which a single person or thing makes an appearance (in other words, with intransitive verbs), the words 'subject' and 'object' are inappropriate. The terms *agent* and *patient* are used instead. This is not mere pedantry – these words have a different meaning from 'subject' and 'object'. Both of the two sentences discussed so far – 'I call her' and 'I hesitate' – have a patient: the woman being called is a patient, but the man who is hesitating is a patient too. Hesitating, the Basques consider, is not something you do; you undergo it, passively – hence 'patient'. (*Passive* and *patient* both derive from the Latin verb *pati* meaning 'to suffer'. Along with *passion*, oddly enough.) An agent is present only in the sentence about the phone call: he is the caller.

Basque case markings reflect this distinction: all agents are in the same case, and all patients. But these cases are not the 'nominatives' and 'accusatives' of so many other European languages, including English: *I* and *she* are nominatives, *me* and *her* are accusatives. Basque cases are different beasts entirely: there are *ergatives* (for the patient) and *absolutives* (for the agent). As in German and Russian and Latin, every noun has to be marked for case, but even Germans and Russians find it hard to wrap their heads around Basque, because the logic of the cases is nothing like their own. So if you feel a bit bewildered, don't worry: you're not alone. Ergative languages take a lot of getting used to.

Obviously, English is not an ergative language; it's an accusative language. But this doesn't mean that ergativity is entirely absent from English. There is a group of verbs called 'ergative verbs', which behave in a way that has affinities with the Basque system. One example is *to break*. If I break a glass, I could report the situation as 'I broke the glass' or as 'The glass broke'. In both cases the glass is the patient: it hasn't *done* anything, but someone has done something *to* it. Typically, the patient is the object of English sentences, not the subject (except in the passive

ABDEFGHiKLM NÑOPRSTUXZ

THE BASQUES USE A REGULAR ALPHABET BUT THEY FAVOUR THEIR OWN RATHER CIRCUS-LIKE FONT, BASED ON STONE CARVING.

voice, but let's leave that aside). However, with *break* and some other verbs such as *boil, turn* and *drive*, the patient is the object when the agent is mentioned and the subject when the agent is not mentioned. In English, the great majority of verbs do not work that way. You can't simply turn 'I call Jenny' into 'Jenny calls' – the two sentences have a different meaning.

Ergativity seems exotic to us, but that's only because we're European. In South Asia, New Guinea, Australia, the Pacific Ocean and the Americas the phenomenon is widespread. Few of those languages, however, are as consistent as Basque. For example, some of them use the English system for the present tense and the Basque system for the past tense. Or they use our system for 'I' and 'you', but the Basque system for the third person and all plurals. A mixed system like this is classified as 'split ergativity'.

The hard-core, strictly ergative languages are somewhat marginal: they have few speakers (Basque, with under a million speakers, is one of the largest) and are mostly found in isolated areas such as the Caucasus, Greenland, New Guinea and the Amazon basin. But split ergativity can be found in about 20 to 25 per cent of all languages, including big ones such as Hindi, Bengali and the Philippine language Tagalog.

Not only is ergativity far from extinct; research into sign language has shown that it also arises spontaneously. Four

American and four Chinese deaf children of hearing parents have each developed fully-fledged sign languages that include ergative systems. Systems that their mothers, however, were not able to master: they did learn the sign language, but without the ergativity.

Modern Basques do it the other way round: when they start learning Spanish (or French) they have to master a non-ergative system. They have to figure out that in Spanish they can't say 'me calls she', but 'I call her' instead. That, and a whole bunch of other things that are radically different in Spanish and Basque: articles and prepositions that are placed behind the noun, an absence of gender, and much more.

It's quite phenomenal, really, how Basques can handle a 'water language' and a 'mountain language' alongside each other. Apparently, the human mind can be both a swimmer and a mountaineer at the same time.

⇋ The word 'anchovy' was borrowed from Portuguese, but its origin may be the Basque word *anchu* for 'dried fish'.

💡 *Erdaratze* – to translate 'out', from one's own language into a foreign one. The opposite, *euskaratu*, means 'to translate into Basque' rather less useful from a British perspective. For translators and interpreters, the difference in translating in or out is crucial, and tends to require a lot of words for lack of this particular item of vocabulary.

41

Note to self

Ukrainian

Few words have as unequivocal a meaning as *his* and *her*, you might think. *His*: belonging to a male just mentioned (or about to be mentioned, or simply present). *Her*: ditto for female.

But consider this sentence: *Mary punched the policewoman in the face, grabbed her bicycle and raced off.* Ambiguous, isn't it? On whose bike did Mary make her escape? Did she have an environmentally friendly getaway vehicle at the ready, or did she simply pinch the patrol bike of the hapless officer? Of course there are ways to clarify which bike Mary used for her getaway, but they require more words. For example: *Mary punched the policewoman in the face, grabbed her own bicycle and raced off.* We now know that the criminal departed on her own bike, though *her own* might be taken to imply that she had a number of bicycles to choose from. If the bike belonged to the police officer, on the other hand, the most efficient way of expressing that would be to replace the word *her* altogether by something more precise: *Mary punched the policewoman in the face, grabbed the officer's bicycle and raced off.* It's not fine prose, but it's clear.

There are still further methods for clarifying whose bike it was ('grabbed the bicycle she'd brought', 'grabbed the victim's bicycle', 'stole her bicycle', 'seized the latter's bike', and so on), but my point is this: the word *her* – and the same goes for *his* – is not as unambiguous as you might think. When we say or write these pronouns, we have to be on our guard in order to spot potential misunderstandings, and then take measures for avoiding them. Only if the people are of different sexes is there perfect clarity: 'The woman punched the man and jumped on his bike' or 'on her bike'.

Many other languages, such as French, German and Spanish, face this same problem. But others have come up with elegant solutions. Slavic and Scandinavian languages are different from English in this regard. And, dare I say it, better. They simply don't allow for ambiguity like that in the sentence above, because they have a possessive pronoun that we are sorely lacking.

Let's take Ukrainian as an example. This language, too, has words for 'his' and 'her': *joho* and *jiji* (normally in Cyrillic script). If you also happen to know that *beru* means 'I grab' or 'I take' and *velosyped* is 'bike', the following sentences are clear: *Beru joho velosyped* ('I take his bike') and *Beru jiji velosyped* ('I take her bike').

However, if it's not me but rather a third party who grabs the bike, then not only does the verb take a different form – *bere* ('he/she grabs') – but a completely different possessive pronoun suddenly appears: *Bere svij velosyped.* This means 'he/she grabs his/her (own) bike'. While *svij* disregards the question of the actor's gender, it leaves no room for misunderstanding that it's referring back to the subject of the sentence. In the English crime report above, Mary was the subject and the police officer was the object. Depending on whose bike was grabbed, a Ukrainian would use the *svij* (for Mary) or *jiji* (for the officer).

Scandinavians – whose languages are not all that different from our own – also have the use of reflexive possessive pronouns,

UKRAINIAN MAY BE A LESSER KNOWN LANGUAGE IN BRITAIN, YET THIS SIGN IS IN DERBYSHIRE.

to give them their proper name. In Swedish, *sin cykel* can mean 'his (own) bike' or 'her (own) bike', depending on whether the subject of the sentence is a man or a woman. The Scandinavians only use this reflexive possessive pronoun in the third person, but the Slavs go a step further: they also apply it to the first and second person. This results in a perfectly logical system, which nevertheless leaves English speakers thoroughly confused. 'I grab my bike' in Ukrainian is not *Beru mij velosyped*, although *mij* does indeed mean 'my'. The correct phrase is *Beru svij velosyped*, with that same *svij* that we encountered above in the sense of 'his'/'her'. When *svij* refers back to the subject 'I', it automatically means 'my'. Using the same ironclad logic, Ukrainian also has a single word, *sebe*, that does something we need a whole product line for: *myself, yourself, herself, himself, itself, oneself, ourselves, yourselves* and *themselves*. What *sebe* means in any particular case depends on the subject of the sentence.

The precision and concision are admirable. Sadly, though, in English we have no equivalent to the Ukrainian *svij* and the Swedish *sin*, never mind the highly versatile *sebe*. Many hundreds of Scandinavian words made their way into English in the Middle Ages, including such useful items as *egg* and *they* and *oaf*. If only the people of medieval England had had the common sense to adopt this equally useful Scandinavian pronoun as well.

⇆ Ukrainians like to think that 'cossack' is of Ukrainian rather than Russian origin, as the word is written *kozak* in their language as against the Russian *kazak*. Tracing its history further back reveals that the word is Turkic.

💡 *Sebe* – as discussed above – allows a single word for myself, yourself, herself, himself, itself, ourselves, yourselves, themselves.

PART SEVEN

Intensive care

Languages on the brink and beyond

Small languages are not necessarily doomed. It helps if the speakers have full or partial political independence, as in Monaco, Ireland and Gagauzia. Tiny Dalmatian wasn't so lucky, but even death needn't be the last word – two Celtic languages (Cornish and Manx) have been raised from the grave.

GAGAUZIA MOLDOVA

8000

Принцесса Уэльская

...-1997гг.

...родная принцесса

INDONESI

42

Networking in Monaco

Monégasque

It's impossible to feel sorry for the super-rich who set themselves up in the Mediterranean tax haven of Monaco, but you might just about feel a glimmer of pity for their kids when you know what they have to go through at school. Their parents can get by in French or English but the children don't have it so easy – they have to spend seven years at school learning Monégasque.

Monégasque! A minor subdialect of Ligurian, which is itself just a dialect of Italian. A language with around a hundred native speakers, who all speak French most of the time. A language you won't find on the radio or on TV. A language whose literary output amounts to little more than an annual calendar and the occasional reprint of the patriotic poems of Louis Notari, the principality's only notable writer. A language that has to make do without its own version of Wikipedia – an affront not suffered even by Scots or Manx, or indeed many European languages too tiny to have made it into this book, such as Mirandese, Pontic Greek and Võro. A language that not a single official body uses, not even in Monaco. A language, in short, hardly ever spoken by anyone anywhere, except by schoolkids in their Monégasque lessons.

These poor children can blame their ordeal on Georges Franzi (1914–97). This canon of Monaco's cathedral was dismayed by the approaching disappearance of his beloved dialect. Unlike most other speakers of endangered languages, however, Franzi had a trump card: his little black book included none other than Prince Rainier III of Monaco and his Princess Consort, the film star Grace Kelly. And behold, in 1976 it pleased His Serene Highness to decree that lessons in the Monégasque tongue should be mandatory in schools all across the realm (all 0.75 square miles of it).

Of course, one is inclined to applaud any such efforts to sustain an endangered language. But there is a strange irony here. Because in France – the country to which Monaco belongs, to all intents and purposes – no such measures are being taken to preserve the country's minority languages. There, millions of people speak a raft of regional languages: from Basque to Alsatian, Occitan to Breton, Catalan to Flemish. But *lessons* in these regional languages? Not a chance.

⇆ English has no Monégasque loanword – and probably no language has. The English adjective 'Monégasque', which to our eyes has little apparent connection to Monaco, is derived from the local word *Monegascu*.

💡 *Stincu* or *purpassu* – calf (of the leg). It might be helpful if the English word for a youthful cow were not also an anatomical term.

43

A narrow escape

Irish

A near-death experience does tend to have an effect on a person – it's not possible to get a glimpse of the pearly gates and come away unaffected. That's true for any of us, and it's equally true for a language.

Take Irish Gaelic, or Irish for short. Even if it hadn't had its close encounter with oblivion, it would still be an unusual language by any standard. For one thing, it boasts the second oldest literary tradition among living European languages, after Greek. As early as the fifth century, while the continent and Britain were prey to marauding illiterate Germanic war bands, in Ireland learned men were composing poems in the vernacular.

And nor is it just its pedigree that makes Irish special. Linguistically too, it's a whole other kettle of fish. Whereas English and the continental languages of Western and Central Europe have deeply influenced each other, resulting in a set of grammatical features that linguists call 'Standard Average European', Irish developed quite independently. So did the other Celtic languages, by the way, with the partial exception of Breton.

They're recognisably Indo-European, but they stretch the limits of what it means to belong to that family.

Yet another special feature of Irish is its phonology. Of course, most languages have their distinctive lisps, rattles and croaks, but the three Gaelic languages (Irish, Manx and Scots Gaelic, which together comprise a subcategory of Celtic) do something to their consonants that is as unusual as it is hard to describe in everyday terms. Suffice it to say that almost every consonant can be pronounced in either of two ways, and that the meaning of many words is dependent on this.

But how did the near-death experience come about, for such an ancient and individual language?

Like much of Europe, Ireland stopped being entirely monolingual at an early stage: the Christian church introduced some Latin; the Vikings who founded Dublin and other cities spoke Norse; invaders from Britain spoke Norman and English. Yet Irish remained the majority language, and the elites of foreign origin became Gaelicised. In the late sixteenth century, however, the situation changed. England's rulers decided to conquer their western neighbour properly and this they brutally did. By the seventeenth century, they controlled all of Ireland. Rebellion, which was frequent, was bloodily quashed. In the course of a century and a half, a significant proportion of the Gaelic population – one third, according to some estimates – was either killed or forced into exile. Meanwhile the number of English and Scots speakers in Ireland rose, as land was confiscated and given to British colonists. Moreover, new legislation banned Catholics (Gaelic speakers, in other words) from owning or leasing land, voting, obtaining education, entering a profession or even living within five miles of any major town. In a word, the majority of the population was being deliberately impoverished.

The language shift from Irish to English was accelerated in the nineteenth century, largely as a result of the Great Famine.

Repeated potato crop failures led to an emergency that was mismanaged to such an extent that some British politicians spoke scathingly of 'a policy of extermination'. In just a few years about one million people died of famine-related causes and an even larger number escaped their misery by emigrating, with Gaelic speakers heavily over-represented in both groups. The population of the countryside would continue to drop for decades after the famine was over. By the time the Irish Free State was founded in 1922, only a few hundred thousand Irish people spoke Gaelic, out of a population of four million, and most of them were marginal in every respect: poor, with very little education and living in the remotest parts of the countryside.

Was this the moment of Irish Gaelic's near-death? No, it was to get worse. The nationalists had always used the language as a badge of Irishness. Now in power, wanting to revive it at the expense of English, they pursued policies ill-suited to this end. They turned the last strongholds of Irish – a string of scattered communities along the west coast – into a legal entity called the Gaeltacht and hoped that the language would reconquer the country from there. To speed up the process, attempts were made to Gaelicise education throughout the republic. But lacking textbooks and qualified teachers, the project was never a success. Eventually the preference for Irish as the language of instruction was abandoned in favour of compulsory Irish lessons, with all other subjects taught in English.

It is a surprising fact that most people in those days only encountered Irish at school. Outside the Gaeltacht, official communication (even signposts), education, church services and the media were, with very minor exceptions, English-only. As a result, Irish became established in most people's minds as the language of the past, a symbol of an idyllic Celtic yesteryear, rather than a language fit for the present day, never mind for the future.

The Gaeltacht, meanwhile, began to integrate into an Ireland that was rapidly modernising. The availability of affordable property drew English speakers into the pretty rural communities, where the default language, in public, duly became English. Some of the Irish speakers, conversely, moved to the towns in search of work, and stopped raising their children in Irish. In the 1970s, the language seemed set for extinction. When Ireland joined the European Community in 1973, the government didn't even demand that Irish be added to the list of Europe's working languages.

This was the low point – the near-death experience. A colonial bully had beaten Gaelic to a pulp, then an inept nationalist doctor had failed to save it. The end seemed to be inevitable. A language that's sustained by the classroom, rather than by daily conversation with family, friends and social contacts of all sorts, is living on borrowed time.

What saved Gaelic was bottom-up activism. It was not only native speakers who rescued it, but also, and increasingly, 'linguistic converts' – English speakers who took action to reverse the historical language shift. The Gaeltacht might have been becoming ever less Gaelic, but Ireland as a whole now began to move towards bilingualism. In 1972 a nationwide radio service in Irish was established. At the same time the number of *Gaelscoileanna* – schools with Irish as their instruction language – began to increase; they now make up some 15 percent of all Irish schools, and roughly half of them are outside the Gaeltacht. In 1997 came the launch of a Gaelic TV channel, *Teilifís na Gaeilge* (now TG4). In 2003, it became compulsory for public bodies to communicate with the public in both official languages. And in 2007, Irish was classified as an official EU working language.

But as I said, a near-death experience does something to you, and it did something to the Irish language. Of the 90,000 or so people for whom Irish is part of their daily lives, an increasing

CYCLING IN THE GAELTACHT – YET ANOTHER UPHILL STRUGGLE.

number are urban, highly educated second-language speakers, and their Irish is, well, just not quite the same as the old language. Some politely call it urban Irish. Others mock it as 'Gaelscoil' ('school'), 'broken' or even 'pidgin' Irish.

The differences are quite significant. Linguist Brian Ó Broin observed a few years ago that urban second-language speakers had trouble understanding native speakers, whereas native, mostly rural speakers found the Irish of urbanites jarring on the ear. He looked into the matter more closely and realised that urban speakers were simplifying two of the language's most distinctive features, one phonological, the other grammatical. They're not doing it consistently yet, but the tendency is clear.

Just to see how startling this discovery was, let's try to imagine similar changes in English. On the phonology side, imagine that a substantial and growing group of speakers were to stop distinguishing between *rib* and *rip*, between *bag* and *back* or between *raise* and *race*. As for grammar, let's propose they start making many strong verbs weak, so that, for example, they would report how their team's hopes had *rised*, but after their opponents had *winned*, they had *throwed in* the towel. Traditionalists would shudder at these 'innovations'. The innovators, on the other hand, might start to have some trouble decoding words like *torn*, *bred* and *underwent* when listening to old-school speakers. They would say *teared*, *breeded* and *undergoed*.

You may argue that these innovators are nothing of the sort and should simply get their act together. But language change is nothing if not democratic. As soon as sufficient numbers of people feel that the past tense of *dare* is *dared*, the original form *durst* will vanish (as indeed it has), regardless of the pain this causes the old-schoolers. Usually, these sorts of differences appear between generations. But with Irish, the rift is rather between rural and urban speakers. And since numerically the former are on the decline and the latter on the rise, the innovations stand an excellent chance of becoming the new norm.

So is it correct to claim that Irish, having been nearly dead, is now resurgent? In a way, yes. But perhaps it would be more exact to say: Gaeltacht Irish is dying, Gaelscoil Irish is taking its place.

⇄ Among the words borrowed from Irish are 'slew', 'galore' and 'trousers'. It's often hard to distinguish between Scottish and Irish Gaelic loans.

💡 *Bothántaíocht* – the act of socialising by going from house to house.

44

No laughing matter

Gagauz

Just admit it: to English ears, 'Gagauz' is a word that's hard to take seriously. It sounds like baby talk, it sounds like Lady Gaga, it sounds like all sorts of things – but the one thing it doesn't sound like is the name of a language. Could this be a matter of habituation, nothing more? Would names such as Finnish and Czech (think 'photo finish' and 'traveller's cheque') sound equally odd if we didn't hear them on a regular basis? Conversely, would we quickly get used to languages with names like Gagauz, Balochi and Mazandarani if we went on holiday to places like Gagauzia, Balochistan and Mazandaran?

Maybe. But the Gagauz people – as the speakers of Gagauz are called – have themselves not always been happy with the name. In the past they referred to themselves as 'Greeks' (although they didn't speak Greek) or 'Christian Bulgarians' (which was neither specific enough, since most Bulgarians were Christians, nor altogether appropriate, as they didn't speak Bulgarian). When the real Bulgarians began calling them 'Gagauz' in the nineteenth century, they saw it as an insult. Still, when in 1994

STAMPS ARE A BIT OF AN INDUSTRY IN GAGAUZIA – AND THEY HAVE
WIDE AND SOME MIGHT SAY BIZARRE TASTES.

they at last managed to acquire an autonomous region in
(Romanian-speaking) Moldova, they called it Gagauzia; the name
had evidently lost its bite.

Within this young territory, which is just slightly larger
than Greater London, the majority of the population consider
themselves Gagauz. Around 150,000 people speak the language,
which is closely related to Turkish. This means that, but for a
few Bulgarian and Russian loanwords here and there, it is easy
enough to follow for speakers of Standard Turkish. However, just
as Germans find Dutch comical, and the Dutch in turn can't help
but snigger at Afrikaans, the Turks sometimes have to suppress
their giggles when it comes to Gagauz.

The fun lies in a handful of grammatical subtleties that
Gagauz has incorporated from two Slavic languages, Bulgarian

and Russian. One is the word order: in Gagauz, the direct object comes after the verb, as in 'the child eats (verb) an ice cream (direct object)'. The Turks find this terrifically funny, because for them it goes without saying that any person in their right mind would say 'The child an ice cream eats.' Another case of typically Slavic import-humour is the Gagauzian habit of distinguishing between men and women. Why *padişah* for a king, but *padişahka* for a queen? Why don't witches (*büücüykä*) have the same name as wizards (*büücü*)? Ludicrous affectation, according to the Turks. One word is more than enough.

Clearly, what the Turks find so funny is perfectly ordinary for us. For us, Gagauz is no more comical than English – except for the name, of course. And perhaps the stamps.

⇆ ☀ No Gagauz words have been borrowed by English and none that I've come upon seem especially desirable.

45

The death of a language

Dalmatian

It's rare for a language to expire with a bang rather than a whimper, but that's just what happened on 10 June 1898, when a landmine exploded on the Adriatic island of Krk. There were two casualties: a man named Tuone Udaina, and the Dalmatian language of which he was the last speaker.

While Udaina's death was an unexpected calamity, the demise of Dalmatian had been a long time coming. It had developed out of Latin in the area immediately east of the Adriatic Sea, and it was a marginal language almost from the outset, as most of the Balkan region was taken over by Slavs in the sixth century. Dalmatian maintained a toehold on a few islands near Istria and in a handful of coastal cities further south, the most significant being Dubrovnik (or Ragusa, in Dalmatian). Even at its high point, Dalmatian may well have had only 50,000 speakers. Hardly any texts have been preserved, presumably because hardly any were written. In Dubrovnik, it became extinct in the sixteenth century. By the nineteenth, it had been reduced to a minority language on just one island, known as Krk in Croatian and Vikla in Dalmatian.

It was the connection with Venice that helped this small Romance language to cling on to life for so long in the midst of an overwhelming Slavic majority. For centuries Venice was the capital of a far-flung maritime empire which included much of the eastern Adriatic, and the constant interaction with the Venetians must have played a part in sustaining the Romance language of the Dalmatian coast. Venetian sovereignty

THE LUCKLESS TUONE UDAINA, LAST SPEAKER OF DALMATIAN.

over Ragusa came to an end in 1358, but Krk's connection to Venice endured rather longer, and it was here that Dalmatian survived. On 18 April 1797, however, Venice ceased to exist as an independent republic, and from that moment the days of Dalmatian were numbered. It turned out to have 36,942 days left, to be precise.

It wasn't until 1897 that somebody thought it might be a good idea to record this practically undocumented tongue for posterity. In that year, the Italian linguist Matteo Bartoli set out to do this by interviewing Tuone Udaina. Neither man was ideally suited for the task. Dalmatian was not Udaina's first language, he hadn't had occasion to speak it since the death of his parents twenty years previously and his pronunciation was less than crystal clear, as he was by now in his mid-seventies and completely lacking in teeth. As for Bartoli, he was a hard-working expert in Romance languages, but he had his limitations. In the words of the rather greater linguist Giacomo Devoto, 'Taste for phonemics, syntax, stylistics, general grammar, the description of a system in general, remained foreign to him.'

This isn't to say that we could have had a complete and reliable knowledge of Dalmatian if only a more assiduous linguist had been given the opportunity to interview someone with a full set of teeth for a longer time. When a language is down to its last speaker, it is already defunct. Language lives through conversation; a man alone cannot keep it alive – he can do little but recall it, to the best of his ability.

That said, 'the death of the last speaker' is an event of great pathos, and such moments have become something of a media set piece. Language death is happening all the time. It is estimated that some 500 languages worldwide are currently spoken by fewer than 100 people; around fifty languages are spoken by just a single individual. In 2013, the last native speaker of Livonian died in Latvia. In 2012, the last speaker of the Cromarty dialect in Scotland breathed his last. And in 2011, in a welcome variation on the theme, it was reported that the last two speakers of Ayapaneco, in Mexico, refused to talk to each other. A good story, that was. But in terms of drama, it will be hard to surpass the standard set by Dalmatian.

⇆ No English words were borrowed from Dalmatian. The Dalmatian dog is named after the region, but it's uncertain if the breed originated there.

💡 *Vu* – you (plural). This is a glaring gap in the English language. *Vu* sounds like French *vous*, which means the same thing.

46

The church of Kernow

Cornish

Is Cornish a living language? Well, that's largely a question of faith. Until recently, unbelievers could invoke the UNESCO atlas of endangered languages, which listed Cornish as 'extinct'. This was not overly surprising, given that the woman who is widely held to be the Last True Native Speaker – one Dolly Pentreath, a fish-seller from Mousehole – died in 1777. True, a man by the name of John Davey, who died in 1891 at the age of 79, knew some Cornish words and phrases that he had learnt as a boy from his father, but it's not clear how much of the language he had ever spoken. A few people with some grasp of Cornish even outlived John Davey, but again they didn't really speak it. Dolly Pentreath does seem to have been the last one.

The true believer, however, does not accept that death is the end of the story, and since the late nineteenth century there have been many attempts to revive the language. Today, with the resources of the internet, resurrection has become more feasible than ever, even if one is obliged to spread the word by using the global language rather than the local one: the Cornish portal www.magakernow.org.uk, which hails Cornish as 'the mother tongue of the region', is almost entirely in English.

English remains the first language of Cornwall, but the 'mother tongue' is in rather better health than it used to be. Since the early twentieth century, thousands of people have learned to speak Cornish, which has resulted in a community of several hundred people who now use it for everyday purposes. Other languages, such as Manx (see following chapter) have similarly eluded extinction, but something makes Cornish exceptional among resurrected languages: its proponents have disagreed as to exactly what they should be reviving.

While the first influential revivalist, Henry Jenner, quite sensibly based his 1904 handbook on the language that had been spoken and written in the century leading up to its demise, his pupil Robert Morton Nance took a more radical stance. Cornish had seen its literary prime in the late Middle Ages, he argued, so let's revive the language as it was spoken then. Not only was his spelling rather different from Jenner's, Nance also introduced a lot of old words that Dolly Pentreath and her contemporaries wouldn't have recognised. Nance's creation came to be known as 'Unified Cornish' (UC or *Kernewek Unys*), and it remained the Cornish standard until the 1980s.

In the late twentieth century, several new denominations of Cornish sprang up, with names such as Common Cornish (CC, *Kernewek Kemmyn*), Unified Cornish Revised (UCR, *Kernowek Unys Amendys*) and Modern or Revived Late Cornish (RLC, or *Kernuack Nowedga* or *Kernuack Dewethas*). All tried to make the spelling more regular, but in different ways. They also disagreed over the best model for Cornish: should vocabulary, grammar and pronunciation reflect the late medieval, the sixteenth- or the eighteenth-century variety?

What they did agree on was that schisms were undesirable. Consensus became particularly urgent after 2002, when the

STRANDED, BUT HOPING FOR ANOTHER HIGH TIDE. NOTE CORNISH FLAG.

British government recognised Cornish – no variety was specified – under the European Charter for Regional or Minority Languages. The factions began an ecumenical process, and in 2008 they announced that they had agreed on a compromise, called Standard Written Form. The official translation of this English name is *Furv Skrifys Savonek*, but UCR speakers prefer *Form Screfys Standard*. Unification isn't a straightforward business.

Dissidence may not have been entirely eradicated, but Standard Written Form is now the variety of choice for anyone wanting to learn the language of Kernow. In terms of pronunciation, SWF occupies a middle ground between existing standards. This may be sensible, but it means that contemporary Cornish is pronounced unlike any earlier variety of the language. The vocabulary shows the same spirit of compromise: the dictionary gives many synonyms, some preferred by the 'medievalists', others by the 'modernists' (those who prefer eighteenth-century Cornish). Sometimes, these synonyms are simply a product of the changes in pronunciation that took place after the Middle Ages. For instance, the old word *penn* ('head', 'end', 'top') is written and pronounced *pedn* by modernists. In other cases, the differences are more marked: medievalists, for instance, use *pennskol* for 'university', while modernists say *universita*, just as Dolly Pentreath might have done. With modern concepts, too, there tends to be disagreement, with some going for new coinages in purest Cornish – such as *plasen arhansek* or 'silvery disc' – while others prefer loans such as *cidi* or 'CD'. Sometimes, life will trump doctrine, and English will impose itself regardless of dictionaries: while 'chips' has two varieties – *asklos* and the more modern *skobmow* – some Cornish speakers will order *chips* without batting an eyelid.

Has the Standard Written Form promoted faith in the language? It seems so. UNESCO has accepted its rebirth and adjusted its own atlas accordingly: Cornish is now listed as 'critically endangered'. And in March 2014 a government subsidy of £120,000 was given to the main Cornish language organisation. The 2008 compromise seems to have paid off nicely.

⇆ 'Gull' is a Celtic loanword, and the most likely lender is Cornish, which has *guilan*. 'Puffin' is also a possible Cornish export.

💡 *Henting*, which means raining hard, is useful for a Cornish holiday, and gets to the *zuggans*, the essence of a thing. *Zuggans* derives from the Cornish *sugen*, meaning 'juice' or 'essence'; *henting* is not (Celtic) Cornish, but rather Anglo-Cornish dialect.

47

Back from the brink

Manx

The Isle of Man is situated in the middle of the Irish Sea within sight of England, Scotland, Ireland and, on a good day, Wales. It should be no surprise, then, that until about 200 years ago the local language was Manx Gaelic, a Celtic language related to Irish and Scottish Gaelic. After the Vikings settled on the island around the end of the first millennium, the Manx language managed to hang on. Against the British, however, it fared less well. In the 1640s the Isle of Man was under the control of the Earl of Derby, whose clash with the Manx militia of William Christian (Illiam Dhone, in Manx) marked the beginning of a lengthy conflict between the Anglophone ruling class and native Manx speakers. Then tourism showed up. The influx of British holidaymakers in the nineteenth century might have brought a lot of very welcome revenue to the impoverished island, but the invasion accelerated the decline of Manx Gaelic. If you wanted to keep the customers happy, you had to speak English.

Soon, Manx was no longer even considered *çhengey firrinagh* ('a real language') and was therefore *cha nel eh feeu loayrt* ('not worth speaking'). 'You'll never earn a penny from her' was the common refrain – *Cha jean oo rieau cosney ping assjee*. Three generations ago, teachers would send schoolchildren to the dunce's corner to do penance for speaking Manx in class. By the 1950s, of roughly 70,000 inhabitants, only two were native speakers of Manx, and both were in their eighties. The other 58 people who had some knowledge of Manx were all adult learners. In 1974, with the death of Ned Maddrell (Ned Beg Hom Ruy), Manx lost its last native speaker – or rather, almost native, as Ned didn't start to learn the language until he was three years old.

The local variety of English of course retained some of its Celtic peculiarities, as it still does. For example, you can't spend an hour on the island without hearing the word 'yessir', which is generally used at the end of sentences as a mild form of assertion, as in 'That's a nice dog you've got there, yessir.' This looks and sounds like 'yes, sir', but in all likelihood it's an English rendering of *uss*, a Manx Gaelic word for 'you', equivalent to the French *toi*. Likewise they say that 'there is good English at François' ('François speaks good English') and that they 'have fallen their keys to the ground', because that's how you'd have put it in Manx. That said, it seemed that the assimilation of the Manx language had reached its conclusion by the mid-1970s.

Now, however, thanks to the efforts of various individuals and organisations, the language has been yanked back from the brink of oblivion. In 2001, the Bunscoill Ghaelgagh (Gaelic Elementary School) opened its doors, to all of seven pupils. Today it has seventy and is going from strength to strength. And it's a Manx-only zone, which forces parents to study the language themselves to keep up with their children. As one mother says: 'My son doesn't take me seriously when I tell him off in English'.

Some parents are concerned that their children might be starting off on the wrong foot, with a 'niche' language whose grammar bears little relation to that of other European languages.

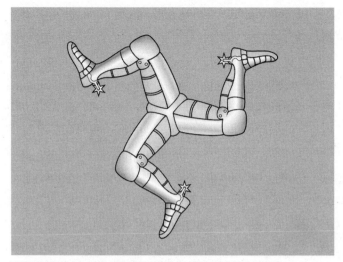

THE MANX FLAG – AN ANCIENT SYMBOL SHARED WITH SICILY.

Yet, according to teachers working with both the Bunscoill and mainstream schools on the island, students at the Gaelic school are picking up French rather more quickly than their peers. And it's not only in French that these students do better – they seem to excel in other subjects, too.

Meanwhile, Manx adults are reconnecting with their native culture and heritage through classes that put the emphasis on speaking the language through imitation, rather than on studying the grammar and vocabulary on paper – there's too high a risk that adults would be dismayed by the sight of language that works so differently from English. No beginner is going to work out the pronunciation of words in Manx Gaelic from the way they are spelt – they are as baffling as the closely related but substantially different spellings of Scottish and Irish Gaelic.

The grammar is even more daunting. And it's not just lenition – that mind-boggling Celtic habit of changing a word's first letter for no apparent reason (see p.189) – that gets to the novice.

For Anglophones, the verb-subject-object sequence of Gaelic languages can take a lot of getting used to. The lack of a verb 'to have' is also challenging. In Manx, you don't 'have' things; they can only be 'at you'. When you have a car, the car is at you; when you speak good Manx, it (or rather 'she') is at you. Even when you have to do something, you say *ta orrym jannoo*, 'it is at me to do'.

There is no 'yes' or 'no' either. When someone asks you a question, you are required to answer with a verb in the correct tense. 'Did you sell your house?' – 'I sold,' and so on. If presented with a trickily complex question, you might weasel your way out by answering *shen eh* ('it is so') – unless it isn't so, in which case you're in trouble, because *shen eh* has no useful negative form.

And yet, against all odds and thanks to the Gaelic school and adult courses, Manx seems to be doing well on its life-support system. Even though the language has only two hundred fluent speakers locally, several new books in Manx are published every year, ranging from murder mysteries to translations of children's classics. There is even a monthly Scrabble event. Of course, the players need a liberal extra helping of the letters y and h, and lashings of vowels. How else are they to compose words like *treechoshagh* ('tripod'), *çhengoaylleeaght* ('linguistics') or *neuymmyd* ('misuse')? And nobody worries if the chosen word is longer than the board; they use the entire width of the table if need be. *Scummey shen* – never mind about that.

....

⇆ No words from Manx have entered standard English. It is sometimes suggested that 'smashing' is derived from *s'mie shen*, meaning 'that's good', but this is very unlikely.

....

☝ *Tayrn* – to carry, heave, haul, drag, pull, pluck, yank, tug, tow, trawl, hitch, draw along, cart or get out (and that's only the half of it). A word signifying any physical effort.

PART EIGHT

Movers and shakers

Linguists who left their mark

Languages are quintessentially collective productions - except the artificial ones, such as Esperanto. That said, several natural languages are indebted to the work of individuals, both in establishing how they should be spoken (Slovak, and the Germanic languages) and in determining how they should be written (Macedonian and Turkish). And some older language variants and dialects might have been forgotten if not for the intervention of dedicated linguists (Albanian).

COLLOQVIA

Oder

Christliche Nützliche

Tischreden

Doctoris Mar-

tini Lutheri / so er in vielen Jaren / gegen gelehrten Leuten / vnd
frembden Gesten / vnd seinen Tischgenossen / nach den Heuptstücken vnserer
Christlichen Lehre / gehalten : Erstlich durch Herrn M. Johannem Aurifabrum seligen / fleis-
sig zusammen getragen / vnd in Druck gegeben : Jetzt auffs newe in ein richtige
Ordnung gebracht / vnd also verfertiget / das sie allen Christen sehr
nötig / nützlich / vnd tröstlich / sonderlich zu diesen elen-
den letzten zeiten / zu lesen sind.

Sampt einer newen Vorrede / vnd kurtzen Beschreibung des
Lebens vnd Wandels Herrn Doctoris Lutheri / auch sehr nützlichem Register
am ende dieses Buchs angehenget / aller Bücher vnd Capitel der Göttlichen heili-
gen Schrifft / wo / vnd wenn dieselbigen der Herr Doctor Lutherus
außgelegt / vnd erkleret habe / vnd in welchen Tomis
solche Außlegung zu finden sey.

Quae semel edocuit diuina mente Lutherus,
Hæc retinet veræ grex pietatis amans.

Nicolaus Selneccerus. D.

Johan. 6.
Samlet die vbrigen Brocken / auff das nichts vmbkomme.

Leipzig /

M. D. LXXXI.

1. 2. 3. 6.

48

Ľudovít Štúr,
the hero linguist

Slovak

Modern linguists don't often stray far from the confines of academia. If they ever raise their voices, it's mostly in defence of their theories or their research budgets. On the great issues of their age, they tend not to speak out. Whenever one of them does, he tends to be Noam Chomsky.

This hasn't always been the case. Many nineteenth-century linguists had a nationalist agenda and a penchant for activism, especially in that swathe of Europe that stretched from Finland all the way down to Greece. And the most active nationalist of the lot was undoubtedly Ľudovít Štúr.

Doesn't ring a bell? Of course he doesn't. In Western Europe, he's utterly obscure. His diacritically over-endowed name doesn't help, either, though it's not as hard to pronounce as you might think: 'LOO-du-eet Shtoor' is a good approximation.

Though anonymous in most of Europe, Štúr is a household name in his native Slovakia. Many of his compatriots can recite

ŠTÚR EVENTUALLY GETS HIS DUES ON THE 500 KORUNA NOTE.

his poems by heart. (Writing poetry was what public figures did in those days, much like appearing on television today.) The house where he was born is now a museum*, as is the house where he died. Statues of him are scattered all over the country. When Slovakia briefly had its own currency, in the nineties and noughties, the 500 koruna note carried his portrait. And he wasn't simply awarded an order of merit – he had one named after him.

And yet he must have regarded his life as a miserable failure. In the eventful and hopeful year 1848, his great dreams – to gain autonomy for the Slovaks and to make Slovak a state language – seemed to be on the verge of becoming true, only to be shattered shortly thereafter: Slovakia remained a Hungarian dependency, its language unrecognised. Štúr's indefatigable efforts as a member of parliament, as a political activist, as an advocate of armed resistance even, bore no fruit.

Fate then focused its attention on his family life. First, his brother Karol died, leaving seven children; Ľudovít took care of them. Within two years, his father, his mother and his closest female friend all died. And Štúr himself was next, just two and

---

* He shares this museum with Alexander Dubček, the leading politician of the Prague Spring. Apparently, they were born in the same eighteenth-century house in the small town of Uhrovec, one in 1815, the other in 1921.

a half years later, at the age of forty. He died a most unheroic death: while hunting, he jumped over some small obstacle and accidentally fired his gun. The bullet wounded him in the leg, and he died a few weeks later, on 12 January 1856.

Why, then, all the statues, the museums, the banknotes, the honours? Chiefly because of his one lasting success: the creation of a unified Slovak language. It was after returning from linguistic studies in Germany that he began his work on a new standard Slovak, based mostly on the Central Slovak dialects. So far, the Slovaks had had two literary languages, one Catholic, based on Western dialects, the other Protestant, a somewhat 'Slovakified' variety of Czech. The standardisation was a group effort, involving other linguists and literary figures, but ever since his schooldays Štúr had tended to assume the leadership of any group he cared to join. So it was under his name that in 1846 *Nauka reči Slovenskej* was published, a prescriptive grammar and spelling of Slovak. Meanwhile, he and his companions had used the new language in nationalist poems, newspapers and books. The spelling was modified afterwards – not necessarily for the better – but even so, today's written Slovak is largely as in the *Nauka*. Hence the acclaim: it was Štúr who created Slovak and it was Slovak that created Slovakia, though the latter would be a long time coming.

....

⇆ The 'dobro', a type of guitar, was developed by the Slovak-American Dopyera brothers. *Dobro* stands for 'Dopyera Brothers', but not coincidentally also means 'good' in Slovak.

....

☏ *Proznovit* – to make someone's phone ring just once in the hope that they will call back (or sometimes as a coded message). Surprisingly many languages have words for this practice, e.g. Spanish *dar un toque* 'give a knock'.

49

The father of Albanology

Albanian

The Albanian language of the late Middle Ages: who could possibly get excited about that, other than Albanian scholars? Not only is the subject far from our doorstep, it's also elusive. Not a single surviving text in the Albanian language pre-dates the fifteenth century; in fact, no document so much as mentions the language until 1285.

Which is not to say that Albanian didn't exist before then. At some point in the distant past, it must have split off from the Indo-European family to which almost all European languages belong. For a while it might have gone by the name of Thracian, Dacian, or Illyrian: these languages did exist, and one of them might have been the precursors of modern Albanian. In any case, during the centuries of Roman occupation the Albanians borrowed hundreds of words from Latin, which their descendants still use in transmogrified forms: *bekoj* ('to bless') comes from *benedicere*, *gaz* ('joy') from *gaudium*.

Until the eleventh century the Albanians probably lived as farmers in the interior of the Balkans, further north than their

FOR LINGUISTS, STAMPS SEEM TO BE THE CHIEF REWARD: HERE, ALBANIA
HONOURS ITS LINGUISTIC PATRON, NORBERT JOKL.

present-day lands, with the outside world taking little notice
of them – let alone of how they talked. It was only later that
they managed to acquire a sizeable territory and language area.
Albanian is now the majority language not only in *Shqipëria*
(as they call Albania), but also in most of Kosovo and parts of
Macedonia and Montenegro. Further afield, there are age-old
Albanian-speaking minorities in Greece, Italy, Turkey and almost
all the Balkan countries.

But enough about that – after all, who could be interested in
the history of Albanian? Well, Norbert Jokl, for one. The so-called
father of Albanology was born to Jewish parents in Bisenz
(nowadays known as Bzenec, in the Czech Republic), in 1877.
He was an Austrian, and became a professor of Indo-European
linguistics at the University of Vienna, where he studied – among
other things – Albanian etymology and the linguistic interaction
between Greece and Albania. He was a bachelor, a polyglot and
socially awkward – the archetypal pre-war scholar.

Following Nazi Germany's annexation of Austria in 1938, Jokl was dismissed from the university, on account of being a Jew. To escape further persecution, he applied for the status of 'half-Jew'. This was refused. He tried to get a job abroad, but his efforts were in vain. An Italian colleague tried to help him move – library and all – to Albania. No luck there either. Then, in May 1942, Jokl was deported, probably to an extermination camp in Belarus. Exactly what happened there remains a mystery, but one thing is certain: Jokl died of unnatural causes that very month, or shortly thereafter.

For decades, Jokl's research lay all but forgotten: fifteen hundred pages of texts from the sixteenth, seventeenth and eighteenth centuries lay waiting for someone to show an interest. It was as if, with the murder of Norbert Jokl, the old language of Albania had been widowed. Foreign linguists had little knowledge of modern Albanian, and even less of the old language. And at home, scholars shied away from the documents. Albania was ruled by a communist dictatorship, and the study of pre-Marxist texts was not encouraged. Worse still, these were Catholic texts; Albania had officially converted to atheism in 1967. The Nazis killed the field's leading expert because they didn't like his faith, and the communists ignored the key historical texts because they didn't like the faith of the people who had written them.

Since the early 1990s, Albania has been making its way back to normality. People are permitted once more to take an interest in their own past, and in the history of their language. But who will satisfy their curiosity? Domestic scholars wishing to study the old books face formidable obstacles. Lack of money is one of them, but the Catholic nature of the texts remains an issue too. Raised as atheists, the current generation of scholars have little knowledge of religious matters; what's more, in this part of the world Christianity made way for Islam centuries ago.

Nor is there much interest from abroad. These days, a research proposal with no prospect of any economic return does little to whet the appetites of the academic powers that be. But as Jokl proved, a single man can sometimes bring a research field to life. And now another Albanologist has taken the plunge. His name is Joachim Matzinger, and together with his team leader, the Indo-Europeanist Stefan Schumacher, he has put Jokl's texts back under the microscope. And they have managed to extract some surprising new insights from them. The humble Albanian language turns out to be the origin of the Balkan habit of glueing articles to the end of nouns (as in *housethe* rather than *the house*) and the source of a good number of loanwords in Romanian. And while the latter discovery may not overly excite you, it does cause a good deal of consternation in Romania, where linguists very much want these loans to be from Dacian, a dead language spoken in classical antiquity, rather than from the language of what they regard as the rustic backwater of Albania.

In the form of Matzinger and Schumacher, the old widow has found new Austrian admirers. In a striking turn of poetic justice, they work in Vienna too. If Norbert Jokl can be called the father of Albanology, then Matzinger and Schumacher can surely be called the sons of Jokl.

....

⇆ English has no loanwords from Albanian. Probably the only Albanian word used in English with any frequency is the name of the Albanian currency, the *lek*, which was named after Alexander the Great. Not to be confused with the zoological meaning of 'lek', which is of Swedish origin.

....

☝ *Teze* – maternal aunt; *dajo* – maternal uncle; *hallë* – paternal aunt; *xhaxha* - paternal uncle.

50

An unexpected standard

Germanic languages

Why is it that Danish, Norwegian and Swedish aren't considered dialects of the one language, even though they're similar to the point of mutual comprehensibility? You may think this an odd question. After all, most European countries have a language to call their own. But have a look at the map of early fifteenth-century Europe. The three Nordic countries are there, albeit with borders that are different from today's. But more striking is the absence of a country that you might expect to see to the south: Germany. Instead of one country, it was a patchwork of statelets – in German, a *Kleinstaaterei*, 'small-statery'. Admittedly, there was a German emperor, the nominal head of an empire that included most of current Germany as well as Switzerland, Austria, the Benelux countries, the Czech Republic, Slovenia and considerable chunks of France, Italy and Poland. But this multi-ethnic, multilingual giant consisted of scores of practically independent states. Think EU rather than USA.

Yet this lack of statehood didn't stop the Germans from developing a standard German language well before political unification in 1871. Even Austria and the Germanic part of Switzerland have embraced their neighbour's standard as their own. And here's the really amazing thing: this one language developed in spite of the German dialects being much more diverse than the ones in Scandinavia.

In the fifteenth century, Gretje from Hamburg and Urs from Zurich would have been hard pressed to achieve anything resembling fluent communication, unless both spoke Latin. Urs might perhaps have managed to water down his Swiss dialect sufficiently for southern Germans to decode it, but the result would still have been very unlike Gretje's Low German. In Scandinavia, by contrast, where each country had its own language, the actual differences between these languages were much less obvious than those between High and Low German (names based on geography, not social standing). Moreover, all three had been influenced heavily by Low German in recent times, a process that had increased the similarities. This is not to say that Erik from Copenhagen, Erik from Uppsala and Eirik from Bergen would have been able to chat effortlessly to each other. But travellers in those days were used to overcoming linguistic obstacles wherever they went, and the obstacles facing the three Erics would have been quite easily surmountable.

So how did a politically fragmented Germany overcome its Babel of dialects to create the common language of Goethe, Wagner and Merkel, a language now spoken by some 100 million people, while a much less fragmented Scandinavia, with just over 20 million inhabitants, ended up with at least three standards? Let us go back to fifteenth-century Germany. What *would* one have expected to happen to its many regional languages? On the face of it, there were no candidates for future supremacy. With the economic prominence of the north waning, Low German was past its prime. In the east, there was a big single-coloured chunk on the map, ruled by the Habsburgs, but this area was

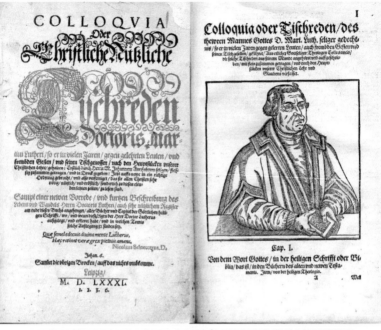

A GERMAN BESTSELLER: MARTIN LUTHER'S *TABLE TALK*, FROM AN EDITION OF 1581. LUTHER DID MUCH FOR THE UNIFICATION OF THE GERMAN LANGUAGE, WHICH GERMANS WERE DESTINED TO READ IN BLACKFACE GOTHIC FONTS UNTIL THE 1940S.

multilingual (German, Czech, Slovak, Slovene and Italian), so it was not best placed to become the cradle of a unified language. On the periphery of the *Kleinstaaterei*, the dialects were just too eccentric: Swiss was hopeless, as was Dutch, which was thought of as German (*Deutsch*) at the time.

Yet there was a lot of cross-boundary communication going on between all these small, tiny and minuscule German states, so there was a need for a linguistic compromise, and it was in the geographic heart of the German lands, such as Hesse, Saxony and Thuringia, that such a compromise was likeliest to be found. Of these three, Saxony was politically the strongest by far, and the written standard (or 'chancellery') language that developed at the Saxon court in the late 1400s was thus a strong candidate for dominance. But there were strong rivals, notably the court languages of Prague and Vienna, and of the peripatetic Imperial Court. These were based on southern dialects, and therefore less palatable to the northern Germans, but their political clout was considerable. At this point it would have been rash to predict that the German language would one day be unified.

What decided the issue was the birth of Martin Luther. Born in the village of Eisleben, he grew up speaking the local Saxon dialect and it was this dialect that was disseminated throughout the German-speaking world when Luther published his translation of the Bible. But does this mean that Germans nowadays speak Saxon? Far from it, in fact; Saxon is the most widely despised dialect in Germany, by a wide margin. This apparent contradiction is easily explained: though the Saxon chancellery language of Luther's Bible language was based on spoken Saxon, its spelling did not precisely reflect the idiosyncrasies of local speech. Spoken Saxon did not distinguish between certain vowel and consonant sounds that were quite distinct in other dialects: where those other dialects had *Blatt* and *Platt*, for instance, Saxon made them sound the same; *Rüben* and *rieben*, likewise, make the same sound in Saxon. Since Luther's spelling became the basis for 'correct' speech, the standard language diverged from the sloppy Saxon pronunciation. As a result, modern German distinguishes between *p* and *b*, *t* and *d*, *ü* and *i*, et cetera.

Martin Luther was the most influential religious figure of his age. It turns out, though, that his Reformation was of even greater scope than you might have imagined: as the biggest-selling author since the invention of the printing press, he also has a claim to being the father of the modern German language.

51

The no-hoper

Esperanto

European languages sometimes make you wonder if they were *designed* to be convoluted and illogical, in order to give their native speakers the satisfaction of being in command of subtleties that few foreigners could ever hope to master. Of course, there is no intention underlying any of the continent's natural languages: Russians didn't invent their madly irregular case system, and Germans didn't choose to have intractable plurals. They simply inherited all this stuff, along with a deep attachment to it.

But Europe does have a language that was created by design, and it's a language whose difficulties might make an English speaker wonder what on earth its inventor was thinking of when he devised it. The inventor was Ludwik Lejzer Zamenhof (1859–1917), and his invention was Esperanto.

It perhaps comes as a surprise to be told that Esperanto is difficult. After all, wasn't it designed in the hope that it would become a practical, easy-to-learn means of communication in a world in which technological advances were bringing nations ever closer together? Wasn't that the reason for its

SHOP SIGNS WRITTEN IN ESPERANTO (THOUGH NOT ENTIRELY CORRECTLY) IN CHAPLIN'S *THE GREAT DICTATOR*.

name, which roughly translates as 'hopeful'? Well, yes, this is all true. And if ever a man was well placed to create such a means of communication, Ludwik Lejzer Zamenhof was that man: not only was he competent in a dozen or so languages, he had the advantage of *not* being a professional linguist. Linguists are excellent at analysis, but they tend to shy away from any interference with the natural course of language development.

Zamenhof must have noticed that of all the languages with which he was familiar, English was in several respects the most learner-friendly. Yet, in concocting Esperanto, he chose to include complexities that might not have foxed his fellow Eastern Europeans (he was born in what is now Poland, to Yiddish-speaking parents of Lithuanian descent), but which have baffled speakers of English ever since.

What makes Esperanto such a challenge for Anglophones? First of all, it has a case system. When a man does something in Esperanto, he is a *viro*: *la viro vidas hundon*, 'the man sees a dog'. But when the roles are reversed, he turns into a *viron*: *la hundo vidas viron*, 'the dog sees a man'. (The dog, you will notice, undergoes the same transformation.) This may not be awfully difficult, but it takes a lot of getting used to for those of us not accustomed to cases – that is, nearly everyone north, west and south of Germany. (And for speakers of French, Italian and Spanish, *la viro* sounds plain wrong. *Il viro* or *el viro* would be OK – but *la viro*? Why the sex change?)

Secondly, Esperanto does odd things to adjectives. 'The beautiful girl', for example, is *la bela knabino* (again, this is odd in itself – *knabino* looks masculine), but when there are two girls an ending is slapped not only onto the girls – turning them into *knabinoj*, a word hardly compatible with anything of beauty – but also onto their attribute: *belaj*. And stranger still, the article remains unchanged: *la belaj knabinoj* 'the beautiful girls'. As far as I'm aware, not a single European language does likewise.

Then there are the verbs. In the early chapters of *Esperanto Without Tears*, Zamenhof seems to have done a great job with them. They're regular, they're simple – they appear to be a breeze. But once you advance beyond the basics, it turns out that the Esperanto verb has some nasty tricks up its sleeve, and the participles are possibly the worst of them. In natural European languages, participles tend to come in two varieties: an active, such as *seeing*, and a passive, such as *seen*. Esperanto verbs have six – three in the passive, three in the active. Thus 'giving a talk' is expressed as *parolonta*, *parolanta* or *parolinta*, depending on whether the talking is still to be done, is in progress or has finished.

And on it goes, from one oddity to the next. Rather than 'She wrote that she would return', the Esperanto equivalent translates as 'She wrote that she *will* return' – unremarkable to Eastern Europeans, but anomalous to Western ears. Esperanto has the 'h' sound, which is hard to pronounce for speakers of Romance languages such as French. Esperanto has consonant clusters like 'str' and 'kl', which has Turks, Japanese and many others tying their tongues in knots – something of a hindrance for a language of supposedly global utility. Worse still, Esperanto has the 'x' sound, the saliva-raking noise of *Bach* and *loch* and a Merseyside *book*, which most English speakers tend to balk at.

All in all, one wonders why Ludwik Lejzer Zamenhof wasn't more radical in making the language easy to learn. He should have made his language a case-free zone – English manages perfectly fine practically without cases. He should have done away with most adverbs – German elegantly substitutes adjectives for them. No verb endings to speak of, either – Chinese gets away with hardly any. No gender, please – Hungarian manages perfectly well with only one word for 'she', 'he' and 'it'. And he should have discarded the 'h' and 'x' sounds, as well as most consonant clusters.

Not that it mattered much. Esperanto, lacking a state and an economy of its own, could never hope to achieve a breakthrough. The world ended up speaking English instead. Which suits the readers of this book, perhaps. As for the rest of the world – we'll come to that in a few pages.

....

⇆ The Esperanto vocabulary is partly based on English (*birdo* for 'bird', *jes* for 'yes', et cetera) but no Esperanto words are found in English, except the proper noun 'Esperanto', of course.

....

💡 *Esperinto* – somebody who used to be hopeful, but no longer is. A word that sums up neatly the mood of most Esperanto speakers.

52

The national hero who wasn't

Macedonian

Saint Cyril was a Macedonian. This is why the Macedonian language is written in the Cyrillic script that he designed, together with his brother Saint Methodius. At least, this is what the Macedonians would have us believe. And there is a kernel of truth to it. But that kernel is buried under a mound of mistakes, misunderstandings and inaccuracies.

To start with, Cyril's name wasn't Cyril, but Constantine. It wasn't until shortly before his death in 869, or perhaps even afterwards, that he was given the name under which he is now known. But that's just the tip of the iceberg.

Diving below the waterline, we discover that he has a rather tenuous connection with the territory now occupied by the Republic of Macedonia, and that he was not actually born into the Slavic language known as Macedonian. Constantine came from the historical region of Macedonia, the kingdom of Philip II and his son, Alexander the Great, which covered parts of present-day

Bulgaria and Greece as well as the Former Yugoslav Republic of Macedonia, as the Republic of Macedonia is now obliged to call itself, following objections from the Greeks, who – unlike the ancient Greeks – insist on regarding ancient Macedonia as part of the ancient Greek world. Specifically, he came from the Greek city of Thessaloniki, and his mother tongue was Greek.

Some time in the distant past, long before Cyril's lifetime, there had been a Macedonian language; this was the language spoken by Alexander the Great. It must have been related to Greek, the language that supplanted it before Slavic tribes descended on the region, in the sixth century AD. At that time the Slavic tongues that were spoken across much of Eastern Europe were still mutually comprehensible, but in the ensuing centuries they developed in different directions. What the Slavic Macedonians ended up speaking was for a long time referred to as Bulgarian. It was not until the early twentieth century that Macedonians began to think they might have their own language, distinct from that of their Bulgarian neighbours, and only in the 1940s was a standard language established, with its own dictionaries and grammar books. As far as their Bulgarian neighbours are concerned, however, the Macedonians are just speaking a Bulgarian dialect.

One indisputable fact is that contemporary Macedonians write their language in the Cyrillic script. And Cyrillic is named after the Macedonian saint; that too is clear. However, Cyrillic was designed not by Cyril, but by his successors at the so-called

THE GLAGOLITIC ALPHABET, DESIGNED FOR AN UNHURRIED AGE.

Preslav Literary School in Bulgaria, several decades after his death. When Cyril (or, more precisely, Constantine) and his brother Methodius (who was known as Michael in his day) translated parts of the Bible into Slavic (although this was not their first language), they used what is known as the Glagolitic alphabet (the alphabet depicted on the previous page). To protect the literary honour of the saintly brothers, it has subsequently been claimed that they must have designed *that* script, in any event. But they probably just added a few characters to it, if that: there are strong indications that the Slavs already had writers before Constantine and Michael embarked on their translation. A translation that they produced, incidentally, not in Macedonia, but much further north, in or around today's Czech Republic.

And so we return to the start of the story, which, as it turns out, should read as follows: 'Constantine was a Greek. This is why the Macedonian language is written in the Cyrillic script that he did not design, together with his brother Michael.'

Now, that's what accurate historiography sounds like.

....

⇆ 'Macedonia', for a mixed fruit or vegetable salad, is derived from the name of the country. French was the first language to use the name in this way.

....

💡 *Pechalba* – working abroad, particularly with the intention of eventually returning to one's family back home.

53

A godless alphabet

Turkish

A Bible in Hebrew, Greek or Latin is no truer or holier than one in English, Estonian or any other language, dead or alive. Not so with the Koran. Translations of the Arabic original do exist, but they don't have anything like the authority of the original. And since the Koran is at the heart of Islam, the book confers tremendous prestige on both the Arabic language and its alphabet.

As a result, that alphabet has been used by Muslims for writing numerous languages that are unrelated to Arabic, and in the past it was used for many, including Spanish, Albanian, Polish and even one Germanic language, Afrikaans. That this is possible shouldn't come as a surprise: after all, the Latin alphabet has been adopted by many languages unrelated to Latin, many of them not even Indo-European.

However, importing a foreign alphabet is not without its problems. There tends to be a mismatch between the number of letters and their customary pronunciation, on the one hand, and the unique sounds of the language in question, on the other.

This is as true for the Arabic alphabet as for the Latin. But just as Czech (see p.107), among many others, has tailored the Latin script to its needs, so several languages have adapted Arabic to theirs. Persian is perhaps the best-known case in point: it has added four letters to the standard set of 28 to represent sounds that are absent from Arabic. Another major language that used to be written in the Arabic alphabet (including the Persian plug-ins) was Ottoman Turkish, or Ottoman for short.

Ottoman was a strange beast: nobody's mother tongue, but an artefact created for the elite of the multi-ethnic Ottoman Empire, employing the material of three natural languages: Turkish, Arabic and Persian. Not only did its vocabulary have elements of all three, but so did its grammar and pronunciation. To the average Turk, Arab or Persian in the souk, the resulting linguistic chimera was largely unintelligible.

In a sense, the new language levelled the playing field within the empire: any man with ambition, be he of Turkish, Arabic, Persian, Serbian, Albanian or any other extraction, had to learn it if he wanted to get anywhere. But it had several drawbacks, and one of them was the alphabet, which was unsuitable especially for the Turkish part of its vocabulary.

Its main flaw was that it contained only three letters to indicate vowels, and even these doubled as consonants. This was not terribly convenient when writing Arabic or Persian, both of which have six vowel sounds, but was even worse in the case of Turkish, which has eight. And since Ottoman contained bits and pieces of all three languages, the meaning (and hence pronunciation) of a word could often only be inferred from context.

Take the letter *waw* (و), for example. It represented a 'w' or 'u' in Arabic, but had to carry the burden of three more vowel sounds in Turkish words: 'ü', 'o' and 'ö'. Some other letters, both vowels and consonants, also stood for more than one sound. All

QWERTY, BUT NOT QUITE AS WE KNOW IT, ON A TURKISH KEYBOARD.

this, added to many vowels not being written at all, made for a lot of ambiguity. The letter combination *kl* (or rather, کل) is a good example. This was the correct spelling for no fewer than eight Ottoman words – four of them Turkish, two Arabic and two Persian – which sounded as differently as 'kel' and 'gül' and had meanings as diverse as 'clay', 'rose', 'all' and 'lassitude'. Thousands of other spellings similarly left readers groping for the sense.

In the mid-nineteenth century, much of the Ottoman elite came to feel that the empire was lagging behind the rest of Europe, where one of the most significant social advances was the rise of mass literacy. In Turkey, many saw the inadequate alphabet as one of the obstacles to modernity. It was suggested that new diacritics should be added to the alphabet, so that the eight Turkish vowels as well as some cumbersome consonants would become unequivocally clear. But no single proposal gained acceptance. The Ottoman authorities would keep dithering over the spelling issue until their fall from power in 1922.

The last sultan was then succeeded by the first president of the new republic, Mustafa Kemal Atatürk, and he was anything but a ditherer. Presiding over a country that was much less diverse than the old empire had been, he dropped Ottoman in favour of a language that was more closely akin to the Turkish of

Istanbul. But this made the spelling question all the more urgent, as any text would now contain more genuinely Turkish words than before, and these were the most difficult to tell apart in Arabic script. But what to do about it?

The idea of introducing the Latin script held little appeal, and not only to conservatives, who despised the 'infidel scratchings'. The Kemalist modernisers, for all their love of Europe, disliked the idea of a spelling modelled on French, the pre-eminent European language in Turkey at the time. They didn't relish the idea of writing the word for 'child', pronounced as 'chojuk', as *tchodjouk* or even *tchodjouque*, or writing 'answer' ('jayvahp') as *djévape* or *djévabe*. For an alternative, some nationalists advocated the Old Turkic alphabet, which somewhat resembles Scandinavian runes and was used by Turkic speakers in pre-Islamic times. Even in these early years of the Kemalist republic, the most realistic option, it seemed, was a reform of the Arabic script.

Yet on 1 November 1928, the Turkish Parliament agreed to replace the Arabic alphabet wholesale with the Latin, albeit under the name of 'Turkish alphabet'. It consisted of the familiar 26 letters minus *q*, *w* and *x* (though they're used in foreign names) plus a few extras: *ç*, *ğ*, *ı* (dotless i; the dotted *i* has *İ* for a capital), *ö*, *ş* and *ü*, making 29 in all. On 1 December 1928, all newspapers converted to the new script and on 1 January 1929, all book printers had to follow suit. Public use of the Arabic script was henceforth forbidden, except in the mosque.

Atatürk himself was responsible for the U-turn, and it was he who chaired the official 1928 spelling commission. He had two reasons for 'going Latin'. One was political: the overall goal of the Kemalist reforms was to create a secular European state, and doing away with the alphabet of the Koran powerfully symbolised this. If the new alphabet rendered illegible to future generations all that had been written in the days of the Ottoman Empire, Islamic and oriental as it was, so much the better.

The other reason was that writing Turkish in Latin letters had become a lot more feasible and attractive. The Soviet Union had just introduced Latin spellings for its many Turkic languages, such as Azerbaijani, Tatar and Turkmen. These, too, had formerly been written in Arabic and here, again, the political aim was to cut the speakers off from the Muslim world. The Soviet linguists had made a good job of it: no trace of French spelling oddities, but a neat sound-to-letter correspondence. However, their alphabets contained several highly unusual characters, such as ə, z, oj and ь, and Atatürk's commission replaced them with ö, j, ğ and ı. As a result, instead of the unwieldy Frenchified *tchodjouk* and *djévape*, Turkish ended up with the crisp and very Turkic *çocuk* and *cevap*.

Incidentally, while Atatürk's aim was to get closer to the modern West, the Soviet leadership didn't like his conversion to the Latin alphabet one bit. They feared that the Turkic peoples within the USSR might politically gravitate towards their linguistic and religious brethren in Turkey. Therefore, in 1939, Stalin banned the Latin script and made Cyrillic compulsory. More than fifty years later, after the dismantling of the Soviet Union, several newly independent republics with Turkic majorities yet again introduced a Latin spelling, this time more in line with that of Turkish. Thus someone born in, say, Azerbaijan in 1915, would have lived through four 'alphabet regimes' by 1995: Arabic, Soviet Latin, Cyrillic and Turkish Latin.

In Turkey, on the other hand, most people have never looked back. Of Atatürk's numerous sweeping reforms, the *harf devrimi* or 'letter revolution' was probably the most successful and, once introduced, least controversial. Its superiority to the old system was just too obvious. The reform is also often credited with the strong rise in literacy that the following decades saw, though of course the new alphabet alone could not have produced such a result. After all, people without schooling can't read and write any language, no matter what spelling it uses.

But if the reform of the Turkish alphabet was intended to hasten the country's integration with Europe, it can't yet be called a success. After all, neither of Turkey's European neighbours have introduced Latin writing: Bulgaria has stuck to Cyrillic, while Greek is unlikely ever to part with its own traditional alphabet. Which might be taken as a symbol of the failure of secular Turks to convince the Europeans that they share a common destiny.

....

⇆ 'Bosh' – in the sense of 'nonsense' – was introduced by the British author James J. Morier; the Turkish *boş* means 'empty'. 'Yogurt' was a direct loan, while 'sorbet' reached English via French and probably Italian.

....

💡 *Nazlanmak* – to feign reluctance, play hard to get.

PART NINE

Warts
and all

Linguistic portrait studies

Having focused on the quirks, histories and splendours of so many languages, let's zoom out and take a broader view of some others: Armenian, for instance, which manages to be strange in many different ways, and the fascinating outliers of Maltese and Faroese. Hungarian turns out to be less exotic than its speakers believe and Finnish is less complex than it might appear, while sign languages are more so. And finally, there's English, a truly weird and wonderful creation.

54

Spell as you speak

Finnish

When it comes to spelling, Finnish is the easiest of all European languages. English is the hardest. Don't believe me? Take a look at the following verse:

If *gh* stands for *p* as in *hiccough*
If *ough* stands for *o* as in *dough*
If *phth* stands for *t* as in *phthisis*
If *eigh* stands for *a* as in *neighbour*
If *tte* stands for *t* as in *gazette*
If *eau* stands for *o* as in *plateau*
Then *potato* should be spelt *ghoughphtheightteeau*

Finns can only laugh at this. Because they write as they speak, and they speak as they write. A Finnish *o*-sound is not occasionally spelt as *oe* ('foe'), *ow* ('low'), *eau* ('gateau') or *ough* ('though'), as it is in English. In all these words, Finns would write *oo*, because they hear a long *o*. And whenever they hear a short *o*, as in the English word *swop* (or *swap*), they write a single *o*. They do likewise with all the other vowels: *a, e, i, u, ö, ä* and *y*. In Inglish, thiiz ruulz wud liid tu spellingz layk this. In Finnish, they

255

produce words such as *suvaitsemattomuus*, meaning 'intolerance', or *happamuudensäätöaineet*, meaning 'food acid'; you do not want to know what the word for 'food acid intolerance' looks like. The disadvantage of these spelling rules, of course, is that Finnish translations are often longer than their originals, as a quick look at any instruction manual will show. But a nation with such an abundance of forests is hardly short of paper.

When it comes to the letters themselves, Finnish is also easier to learn. There is no *c*, *q*, *w*, *x* or *z*, except in foreign words, and even these are often respelled: *pitsa, taksi, kvanttimekaniikka*. *B* and *f* are only seen in loanwords. For a genuine Finnish word, 21 letters suffice (19 common ones plus *ä* and *ö*, which count as separate letters). In other words, five fewer than in English. This amounts to a saving of nearly 20 per cent.

And then we come to word stress. Those who learn English as a foreign language are forced to grapple endlessly with its illogical rules. *P*hotograph is stressed on the first syllable, pho*t*ography on the second and photo*graph*ic on the third. Finnish, however, stresses words on the first syllable. End of story.

What's more, Finnish is a musical language. For every 100 consonants it uses just as many vowels. In contrast, consonants account for 60 per cent of the letters in English texts, which are full of words like *twelfth* and *strings*. And when vowels do appear in English, they are often pronounced as the limp *uh*-sound known as a *schwa*: consider the *a* in *postman*, the *e* in *synthesis*, the *i* in *decimal*, the *o* in *harmony*, the *u* in *medium*, and the *y* in *vinyl*.

Finnish vowels not only sound stronger; they also live together in harmony. 'Dark' vowels, pronounced in the back of the mouth, such as *a*, *o* and *u*, only appear with other back vowels in any given word. Likewise, 'light' or 'front' vowels such as *ä*, *ö*, and *y* also seek out their own kind. That's why 'in the house' is *talossa* (*talo* 'house' + *ssa* 'in'), but 'in the forest' *metsässä* (from *metsä* 'forest' + *ssä* 'in').

THERE'S NO X IN FINNISH. AN 'AXIS' IS AN AKSELI – THOUGH THE X-AXIS IS STILL AN X-AKSELI.

And while we're on the topic of house and forest: those who have tried their hand at German, with its dizzying array of masculine, feminine and neuter nouns might be reassured to know that Finnish words do not present the same problem – whereas a German house is neuter (*das Haus*) and a forest is masculine (*der Wald*), the Finnish equivalents (*talo* and *metsä*) are unisex, like all Finnish nouns. On the other hand, those who enjoy the German language's ability to create new nouns by slamming old ones together will be cheered to know that in Finnish, too, new words are put together just like Lego bricks: *kirja* is a book, *kirjasto* a library. Whole phrases can be constructed in this way. *Taloissani* ('in my houses') consists of four components: *talo* 'house' (we already know that one) + *i* plural + *ssa* 'in' + *ni* 'my'. Thus, Finnish is to be counted among the world's agglutinative (or 'sticky') languages. A beginner's paradise. No endless lists of irregular verbs. No equivalents to the puzzle of why *sing* becomes *sang* whereas *bring* becomes *brought*, or why *try* becomes *tried* whereas *fly* becomes *flew*.

Granted, Finnish also has its dark sides. Fifteen cases. Variable forms of *not*, depending on whether it refers to I, you (singular), you (plural), he/she/it, we or they. And no verb for *to have* – a Finn does not say 'I have a cat' but rather *minulla on kissa*, 'with me is a cat' (which in this instance makes a lot of sense – one never really *owns* a cat). Numerals are a challenge too, because every individual component must receive its own case ending, a procedure that gives rise to lexical behemoths like *kahdestasadastakolmestakymmenestäneljästä* (the sixth case of the word for '234').

But then: *mikään ei ole täydellistä* (22 letters, including 12 vowels). Translation: 'nothing's perfect' (14 letters, only 4 of them vowels).

⇆ Finnish has exported only one word, but what a success it has been: 'sauna'.

💡 *Sisu* – calm and brave determination in the face of adversity. The word has occasionally been used in English since the Second World War.

55

Romans north of Hadrian's Wall

....

Faroese

The Faroe Islands are a handful of bleak, wet and windy rocks, with no neighbours closer than the distant and equally barren islands of Iceland and Shetland. The population is fewer than fifty thousand. No surprise, then, that of all the official languages of Europe, probably not a single one is learnt by so few foreigners as Faroese. The language of the Faroe Islands (where *far* refers to 'sheep' and *oe*, or rather *ø*, means 'island', thus literally the 'Sheep Island Islands') is a job only for those who relish a fruitlessly difficult challenge; the extreme athletes of linguistics, if you like. Unless, of course, you happen to be born there. For everyone else, though, it's a futile enterprise. Even if you should happen to find yourself on the islands, you could chat to the locals in the somewhat more useful Danish language. All Faroese speak it and, to cap it off, with much clearer accents than the Danes.

Besides being useless, the Faroese language is also difficult to learn. With German and Icelandic, it is one of the only three

ANOTHER LINGUIST, ANOTHER STAMP – THIS IS V.U. HAMMERSHAIMB, THE MAN TO BLAME FOR THE WRETCHED FAROESE SPELLING.

Germanic language to have cases – four to be exact. And they are not ones you can get away with mumbling, like German's half-swallowed *dem* and *den* and *der*. These are cases that differ from one another loud and clear, like in Latin. Just as the Romans spoke of *puella* ('the girl'), *puellae* ('the girls') and *puellarum* ('of the girls'), using suffixes to indicate the case, so Faroe Islanders talk about *gentan*, *genturnar* and *gentanna*. Who would have thought it – Romans of sorts, out at sea, far north of Hadrian's Wall.

For the determined, that hurdle may not be too high, especially if you learnt some Latin in school. But then you straight away find yourself facing the next one: in Faroese, spelling and pronunciation share a tenuous relationship. What your eyes see doesn't look like what your ears hear. Of course, this is no different from English. But whereas the English vernacular broke free of the spelling in a gradual and natural manner, the Faroese spelling disaster was effected in one fell swoop by a single man:

Venceslaus Ulricus Hammershaimb. A clergyman and folklorist, Hammershaimb decided in 1846 that his mother tongue should be written as it had sounded centuries before, not as it sounded during his lifetime. As a result, Icelanders, whose language is closely related to Faroese but more conservative in pronunciation, can understand Faroese in writing but not in speech.

Of course, every language can be learnt. For all its quirks, Faroese is still a Germanic language, and thus related to ours: a land is a *land* and a sword is a *svørð*. You just need to take a course to get to grips with it. This, however, is easier said than done. While you can study Germanic languages at many universities, London and Copenhagen are the only European cities in which you can study Faroese. But given the negligible student numbers, it will be a lonely venture.

No, your best bet is a summer course at the *Fróðskaparsetur Føroya*, the local university – literally the 'seat of wisdom'. Here, at least, you can step outside the classroom and immerse yourself in the language community. A community that, unfortunately, has less in common than you might hope, because when it comes to pronunciation the islanders have vastly divergent opinions, though they all agree that you can't be guided by the spelling. For instance, for some the letter *ó* sounds like the *o* in 'dove', for others more like the *i* in 'bird', and for still others like the *ow* in 'fowl'. But there's more: when combined in *ógv* it's a short *e*, as in 'egg'. Except on Suðuroy ('South Island'), where ...

Oh, whatever. Learn Sorbian or Basque instead. They'll be of more use to you.

....

⇆ 'Maelstrom' is a word common to several Germanic languages, but its origin may lie in the Faroe Islands and their language.

56

A meaningful silence

Sign languages

When I told my friends I was taking a sign language course, their reactions surprised me in two ways. Firstly, they showed way more interest than they did when I told them that I was taking lessons in Danish, Spanish, Russian, Norwegian, Romanian and Czech. (No, I don't speak these languages.) And secondly, though my friends are mostly quite a bright bunch, when it came to sign languages their remarks were often rather obtuse. It turned out that for all the missionary work that sign language experts and advocates have done since the early 1980s, most of the old misconceptions still persist. Therefore, this chapter has a straightforward aim: to help set the record straight by correcting seven widely held but erroneous beliefs.

1. 'SIGN LANGUAGE IS INTERNATIONAL'

Ah, would that it were. The course that I took was a primer in Dutch Sign Language (NGT, *Nederlandse Gebarentaal*). Were I to inflict my broken NGT on British signers, they would have a lot of trouble understanding me, because their language of choice would be BSL (British Sign Language), which is unrelated to NGT. Two deaf people fluent in two different sign languages will be able to bridge the gap more effectively and gracefully than two hearing people in different spoken languages, but this is mostly because fluent signers are better at impromptu gesturing. As long as they wish to talk about concrete things, they'll find a way, provided there's sufficient goodwill. As soon as they want to discuss more abstract matters, such as the need for tighter regulation of the financial sector, they will be as lost as the rest of us.

But *why* isn't there one sign language for the whole world? Wouldn't that be much more practical? Undoubtedly. Just as it would make much more sense for the whole world to speak English, or Esperanto, or even Estonian. However, both spoken and signed languages are rooted in communities which have developed a means of communicating among themselves, rather than with the peoples of the wider world. And once communities have a language of their own, it's there to stay. Language shift does occur (look at the case of Ireland), but only under exceptional conditions.

2. 'ENGLISH SIGN LANGUAGE IS THE WORLD LEADER'

With more than 30,000 native users, British (note – not English) Sign Language is a respectably medium-sized language, but certainly not a world language – its Indo-Pakistani counterpart (IPSL) is used by millions. Insofar as any one sign language occupies the position that English has in the speaking world, it's the US variety (ASL). As it happens, this is entirely unrelated to BSL and rather closer to French Sign Language (LSF, *Langue des Signes Française*). The families of spoken languages – Germanic, Romance, Slavic and the rest – are not mirrored in the world of the deaf. Sign language families do exist, but their composition is different because they emerged when educators of the deaf adopted methods and signs from foreign colleagues, who were not always from neighbouring countries. Thus one family grouping includes the sign languages of Sweden, Finland and Portugal, while LSF (from France) is ancestral not only to ASL (USA), but also to ISL (Ireland), NGT (Netherlands) and several others. BSL's next of kin are Auslan (Australia) and NZSL (New Zealand), which resemble BSL so closely that they are considered by some to be dialects of it.

3. 'SIGN LANGUAGES CAN ONLY CONVEY SIMPLE MESSAGES'

Perhaps the most convincing rebuttal of this surprisingly widespread idea is the existence and success of Gallaudet University in Washington, DC, where all subjects – chemistry, accounting, philosophy and many more – are taught and discussed in ASL. This is not to say that every ASL user knows the sign for mercuric chloride or existentialism – but then, most English speakers don't know what these words mean. It doesn't follow that all of the world's sign languages already have a conventional sign for these things – they don't, just as most of the languages of Papua New Guinea, for example, have no words for them. But just as every spoken language can and will develop its lexicon to meet the needs of its speakers, so can, and will, every signed language. And if you think this can't be true because sooner or later they will run out of signs, consider this: is it probable that our tongue, lips and throat are capable of more distinct positions and movements than our arms, fingers and face? The reverse is likelier to be the case.

4. 'SIGN LANGUAGES SPELL OUT SPOKEN WORDS'

Most signs bear no relation to the spoken words of the same meaning. However, signers are able to use spoken (or rather

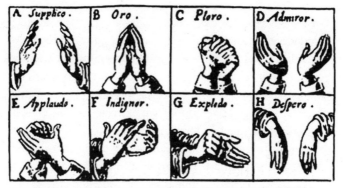

SIGN LANGUAGE 'CHIROGRAMS' FROM THE SEVENTEENTH CENTURY.

written) words by spelling them out in a so-called finger, hand or manual alphabet. This is used only for names and other concepts for which the interlocutors don't have a sign at their immediate disposal. If they need to use the same name or concept repeatedly, signers will find out the conventional sign, having in the interim used finger-spelling or a provisional sign. Again, these alphabets for finger-spelling are not international. As it happens, the British manual alphabet is something of an outlier: while the Irish, French, American, Dutch, German and many other alphabets are one-handed, the alphabet used in Britain is two-handed.

5. 'SIGN LANGUAGES REPRESENT SPOKEN LANGUAGES'

Sign languages developed among people who couldn't hear, so it would come as a surprise if they were direct translations of any spoken language, as indeed they aren't. Crucially, signed sentences have a different structure from spoken sentences (see misconception 6). And – to mention just one other difference – many concepts for which there is a single English word, such as 'small' or 'give', will have more than one sign, often depending on the shape of the object concerned. This is not to say that sign languages exist independently from the spoken languages around them: sign vocabulary is to a degree influenced by spoken vocabulary. Many compound words (apple juice, life insurance, even the sign for 'sign language') follow the same pattern as in the spoken language. Also, part of the vocabulary is accompanied by what's known as 'mouthing', lip movements that often, but not always, noiselessly mimic the corresponding word of the spoken language. Occasionally, different mouthings are the only distinction between two meanings of an otherwise identical sign. Yet on their own, the mouthings are not nearly sufficient to make sense of signed sentences.

Signing systems that reflect spoken languages do exist. Those for English are collectively known as Manually Coded English. These are not fully-fledged and natural languages (hence the word 'system' rather than 'language'), but were designed to facilitate communication between hearing and deaf people.

6. 'SIGN LANGUAGES HAVE NO GRAMMAR'

When I was a child, my mother used to tell me that English has no grammar. What she meant was that in English – unlike in French, German and other European languages – verbs and adjectives have little in the way of grammatical endings. Similarly, and just as incorrectly, it is sometimes claimed that sign languages have no grammar. In fact, sign languages have many grammatical rules. In BSL, questions signs such as 'when' and 'where' come at the end of a sentence and adjectives usually follow nouns – unlike English, which does the reverse. Equally surprisingly, the word order in the Italian Sign Language (LIS) is similar to spoken German, while German Sign Language (DGS) is more like spoken Italian in this respect.

Besides word order, sign languages also have access to a medium or tool that spoken languages do not, namely the three dimensions of space, and they use them to grammatical purpose. 'Asking (a question)', to give a simple example, is always expressed by the same hand shape, but the hand *movement* varies a great deal. In 'I'm asking you', the hand moves from the speaker to the interlocutor. The opposite movement has the opposite meaning.

7. 'SIGNS ARE ICONIC'

The sign for 'apple' looks like biting into one, and in the sign for 'tea' the cuppa is instantly recognisable. These are the visual counterparts of what is known as onomatopoeias in spoken languages: words such as *cuckoo* and *sneeze*, which imitate the sound of the thing that is signified. In sign languages, a much larger number of words are iconic, some of them evidently so, others more subtly. This is simply because gestures are more convenient for representing and imitating objects and actions than sounds are. Yet, even though the collective 'inventors' of sign languages have come up with ingenious signs for many concepts, this still leaves many thousands of other concepts that do not readily lend themselves to iconic representation – how to gesture 'organisation', 'apartment' or 'primrose'? So while sign languages are more iconic than spoken languages are onomatopoeic, an increasing majority of signs are as arbitrary as spoken words.

I could go on: 'Signers can't shout or whisper'; 'Sign languages have no poetry or slang'; 'There's no way of writing down sign languages' – these are all false. Are there no limits then to what sign languages can do? There are a few, just as there are limitations to spoken languages (limited effectiveness in noisy environments, for instance), but signers really have only one major communication problem: the society they live in doesn't share their language. If we were all deaf, we would all sign, and be none the worse for it.

57

Հայերեն Բառակտուծ

Armenian

Armenian is to the family of Indo-European languages what the platypus is to mammals. In both cases, the first glance is enough to raise eyebrows. There's just something uncanny about a creature that has hair *and* a bill. By the same token, the Armenian alphabet – devised by St Mesrop at the start of the fifth century – is unique and somewhat unnerving. In the words of the Russian poet Osip Mandelstam, the letters look like 'blacksmith's tongs'.

They both do strange things, too. The female platypus lays eggs then manages to suckle its young despite a conspicuous absence of nipples (the milk oozes out through pores in the abdomen). As for Armenian, it exhibits what we might call a kind of linguistic kleptomania. Over the centuries it has lifted words indefatigably from the languages of neighbours, rulers and defeated enemies, from Greek and Persian to French, Turkish and Russian. Of its own ancient words – the family heirlooms, so to speak – fewer than five hundred remain. And it's not just words: Armenian plucks sounds from its neighbours too, such as an additional 'glottalic' variant of the *p* and the *k*. That would be like the English starting to roll their r's, as in Spanish, or to talk

ARMENIA HAS BUILT A SPECIAL MONUMENT IN HONOUR OF ITS UNIQUE ALPHABET.

through their noses, like the French. And so modern Armenians speak their own language with a foreign accent, as it were.

The platypus has venom glands like a snake (reptile), 'hibernates' during the summer like some frogs (amphibian), senses electrical fields like a shark or a sturgeon (fish), has a bill like a duck (bird) and suckles on its mother just as we do (mammal). After ample deliberation, nineteenth-century biologists classified it in the latter category, that of mammal. But more recent research suggests it has a fair amount of bird DNA as well.

And Armenian? It has many Persian words, and those glottalic consonants come from the languages of the Caucasus, which are not Indo-European. But in some respects, Armenian also resembles Greek. So after much deliberation, nineteenth-century linguists classified it in its own branch of the Indo-European family, with Greek as its closest living relative. The person behind this move, one Heinrich Hübschmann, faced a great deal of scepticism, because Armenian words often sound nothing like their Indo-European equivalents. For instance, in your average Indo-European language, the word for the number 2 will vaguely resemble 'two' or *duo* or *dva*: first something *d*-like, then something *w*-like and then a vowel. In Armenian, it's *erku*. Totally different word, you'd be forgiven for thinking. But in fact the Armenians have consistently turned the Indo-European initial sound *dw* into *erk*. Thus they fashioned *erkar* ('long') from the old word *dwehro*, and they chewed *hdwon* into *erkn* ('labour of childbirth'). The process seems as implausible as a mammal laying eggs, but facts are facts.

Finally, you might be wondering whether Armenian has any place in a book about the languages of Europe. Armenia, after all, lies south of the Caucasus and this region is classified as part of Asia. But ever since the fourteenth century, considerable numbers of Armenians have been scattered all over Europe – in Russia alone there are more than two million. Venice is home to a famous Armenian monastery, San Lazzaro degli Armeni. There's been an Armenian church in Manchester since 1870, in Amsterdam since 1714, and in Lviv (then Polish, later Austrian and now Ukrainian) since as early as 1370. So the Armenian language has long been part of the European landscape. Hence its inclusion here – under the title *Hayeren Badaktuts*, 'the Armenian platypus'.

....

⇆ English has no loanwords from Armenian, unless you classify as a loan the name of the Armenian currency, the *dram*. Like the dram of whisky, the word originally comes from the Greek *drachmḗ*.

....

💡 *Karot* – a strong feeling of missing someone.

58

Plain lonely

Hungarian

....

'**Please sit down,** Ms Magyar. What can I do for you?'

'I'm just so lonely, doctor. Terribly lonely.'

'I see. And what is it that makes you feel this way?'

'I've not lived in this neighbourhood for all that long. I get the feeling the neighbours don't understand me.'

'Hmm. Let's see, you registered with our practice in ... ah ... oh yes, here it is: in the late ninth century.'

'Yes, that's right. I took over the house where I now live in 896. I don't think the neighbours have ever forgiven me for it.'

'So you're saying there are some old wounds, then. But also that they don't understand you.'

'Yes. We speak a different language. And I have no family either. At least, not close by. My relatives are in Russia, and I've got distant cousins in Finland and Estonia. But I haven't spoken to them in thousands of years; I don't even know if I'd still understand them. I just feel really isolated here on the *puszta*.'

'On the ...? Ah right, the Hungarian plains. Hmm. Ms Magyar, I suspect this issue is too complicated for a primary-care linguist. I'm going to refer you to the hospital for some tests. Here's a referral for the historical linguistics clinic, and one for comparative linguistics. You can call me for the results about two weeks after your appointments.'

'Dr Haspelmath's practice.'

'This is Szabina Magyar. I'm calling for my test results.'

'I'll put you through.'

'Hello, Ms Magyar. I have some good news for you.'

'Oh yes?'

'My colleagues in the comparative and historical clinics conducted some very thorough tests and found that you've become increasingly like your neighbours over the last eleven hundred years.'

'What? That can't be right. Have you ever seen my spelling? And my verb conjugations? And all my different cases?'

'Of course, we took note of all that. But still, the diagnosis holds. To start with, you have articles: you use the words *a* and *az* for "the" and *egy* for "a" and "an". Right?'

'Doesn't everyone use articles?'

'Hardly! Your distant relatives don't, and neither do most languages around the world. But your German and Romanian neighbours do.'

'Oh.'

'Another thing: expressions like "I cut her the nails" instead of "I cut her nails", and "the minister his jacket" instead of "the minister's jacket". You use those as well, right?'

'Yes. Is that special too?'

'Indeed. You don't get that kind of thing in most places, but your neighbours – the Germans and Romanians and Serbians – they do it the same as you. Have done for thousands of years. You got it from them. And there's more. Do you hear anything odd about the words *frigy* for "covenant", *prém* for "fur", *klapec* for "kid", *sztrájk* for "strike", *fröccs* for "spritzer", *pletyka* for "gossip", *próba* for "test", *strand* for "beach"?'

THE MUSEUM OF THE HUNGARIAN LANGUAGE AT SÁTORALJAÚJHELY. ITS
WEBSITE ADVISES THAT 'IT SHOULD BE THE DUTY OF ALL HUNGARIANS
WITH ELEVATED SPIRITS TO MAKE A PILGRIMAGE THERE'.

'No, why? Is there anything wrong with them?'

'Not wrong exactly. But back when you first arrived here,
your words never started with more than one consonant. Your
neighbours' did, though, and now you do, too.'

'Did I? Well, *strand* sounds a bit German. But *frigy*? And *fröccs*?
They don't feel strange.'

'*Frigy* is also from German, Ms Magyar. But you're right, you've
got used to double consonants. *Fröccs* is not a loan, and while
pletyka is from Slovak, it was you who coined *pletykalap* for
"tabloid". And *grófnő* for "countess". *Gróf* for 'count' is almost
German, but *grófnő* certainly isn't. And then there's *világ*. Has it
never struck you as strange that *világ* means both "world" and
"light"?'

'Not really. A coincidence, I guess.'

'Coincidence? Well, your neighbours – except the Germans –
use one word for both meanings. I suppose that's a coincidence

too, is it? And another thing. You say "ice is colder than water", don't you?'

'Well, yes. Ice *is* colder than water, isn't it?'

'I mean, when you compare two things, you attach an ending like "-er" to the adjective, then you say the word *mint* for "than", and only then do you name the thing that's being compared. Which is strange: because you usually put small words like *mint* behind your nouns rather than in front of them. But with *mint* you're copying the neighbours again. Especially the Germans.'

'Is that everything?'

'Not quite. Your superlatives look suspiciously like Serbo-Croatian. But I think I'd better stop, because otherwise it will get too technical. Nominative experiencers and instrumental-comitative polysemy and loss of verbal moods and all that stuff.'

'So what are you suggesting I do?'

'Why not go for a coffee with the neighbours? I'm not really supposed to say this – confidentiality, you know – but I hear your neighbour Romanian is feeling a bit lonely too, what with his whole family being so far away. Why not go and talk to him? There'll be a bit of a language problem at first, but I'm sure you'll find you have a lot in common.'

....

⇆ 'Coach', in all its meanings, goes back to the coach-builders of the Hungarian town of Kocs. And the 'biro' gets its name from its Hungarian-born inventor, László Bíró.

....

💡 *Madárlátta* – food taken for an outing but brought back home uneaten.

59

An Afro-Asiatic in Europe

Maltese

Words from an Afro-Asiatic language are printed on my passport. The same is true of your passport too, if you live in an EU country. Surprised? But it's true: among its many languages, Europe can count one that belongs to the Afro-Asiatic family. Admittedly, the island to which it belongs is just a stone's throw from Africa. But its inhabitants are largely Catholic (though many of these Catholics refer to God as *Allah*), they use the euro, and they can demand communications from Brussels in their own language. Welcome to Malta.

Blessed, or cursed, with a location of great strategic significance, Malta has been frequently invaded, hence the complexity of its linguistic landscape. The Phoenicians gave the island its name: *malat*, meaning 'refuge'. Or was it the Greeks with *melitè*, 'honey sweet'? The Sicilians – who were Arabic Muslims at the time – brought with them an Arabic dialect, which is now the basis of one of the island's two official languages, and the one that's most widely spoken: Maltese. The island later saw off its Norman, German and Spanish masters, only to fall to the

THE HARBOUR AT VALLETTA – NOT A BAD PLACE TO BRUSH UP YOUR
ENGLISH, IF MALTESE DOESN'T APPEAL.

Knights of the Order of St John. They established it as a southern
bastion of the Christian faith, and spiked the Arabic dialect with
Italian words. Then Napoleon showed up, only to be chased away
by the British, who promptly declared their own language to be
the national tongue. Malta has been independent only since the
1960s, and is now finally able to turn the tables by fleecing the
most recent aggressors, the tourists.

And so Malta today is a Catholic island with a Semitic (hence
Afro-Asiatic) language that's written in the Latin script (unlike all
other Semitic languages) and looks a lot like Italian, except for the

odd *ż* and *ħ*, which are typical of Polish and Serbian respectively. (The resemblance to Italian is so strong, in fact, that Mussolini had Maltese classified as an Italian dialect.) What's more, the Maltese speak such good English that exchange students flock from all over the world to brush up their language skills under the blue skies of Valletta rather than the grey skies of London. With such a convoluted heritage, it comes as no surprise that Maltese is one of the few languages in Europe to have, in addition to the singular and plural, a 'dual', inherited from Arabic: while *sena* means 'one year', *sentejn* refers to two years and *snin* to more than two.

And what about the Maltese words on European passports? Some of them won't look too exotic to an English speaker: *Unjoni Ewropea*, *Data* and *Awtorità*, for instance. The same goes for *Sess*. But if you scan the sections headed 'Given names' and 'Place of birth', you'll find that the Maltese words really stand out: *Ismijiet*, *Post tat-twelid*. No mistaking the Afro-Asiatic lineage there.

⇆ Maltese does not seem to have left any imprint on Standard English. But Maltese words, such as *per ezempju* ('for example') and *le* ('no'), are frequently used in Maltese English.

☀ *Ixxemmex* – to bask in the sunshine. Not as in a determined, tan-oriented bout of sunbathing, but as in a casual enjoyment of glorious weather.

60

The global headache

English

English is much like Chinese. I'm not kidding you. The language you're reading right now is in several important ways similar to its sing-song 難以辨認的* counterpart from East Asia. Of course you don't believe it. But it's true all the same. And I'm not talking about anything as mundane as the numbers of people who speak these languages, though that's not a minor similarity. Both English and Chinese have a claim to be the most-spoken language on earth. With China being such a vast and populous place, its language beats all others hands down, if you're counting native speakers only. And while English is a modest number three in the league table of native speakers, trailing behind Spanish, it takes the lead as soon as you include second-language speakers. In practical terms, that's what matters. After all, try finding a local who speaks even the most rudimentary Chinese in Hungary or Egypt or practically any other place. All over the world, English is your safest bet. Anywhere outside the Chinese lands and Chinatowns, of course.

---

* *Nányǐ biànrèn de*: 'illegible, indecipherable'.

But linguistically speaking, numbers are only mildly interesting. When I claim that English is much like Chinese, I have three rather more relevant qualities in mind. The first of these makes either language a poor choice as a world language.* The second one makes them a *very* poor choice as a world language. If anything saves them from being an outrageously poor choice, it's their third shared characteristic.

Number one, then, is their pronunciation. Whether it's English or Chinese whose pronunciation non-natives find it more difficult to learn, it's hard to tell. On balance, I think English takes the biscuit. In the case of Chinese, the problem lies in its tones. Every single vowel must be sung, as it were, otherwise you'll be uttering something silly or even meaningless. This can lead to highly uncomfortable situations. Pronounced in the wrong tone, an innocuous word can turn obscene or offensive. You think you're saying *jī* ('chicken'), but a slip of the tone makes it come out as *jì* and your listener hears 'whore'. Perhaps just as awkwardly, a similar mistake may rob obscenities of their juiciness and make insults sound feeble. As if someone were to call you a 'beach' or a 'son of a beach'.

In practice, Chinese tones are not an insurmountable obstacle. Not to the many Asians and Africans (and the few Europeans) who have them in their own languages, and not even to the many Europeans who don't. After all, we are familiar with changes in pitch – with intonation, as we usually call it. They allow you to express surprise, emphasise certain words or turn a statement into a question, among other things. Speakers of Chinese do likewise, except that their pitch varies at a more rapid pace, serving a different function. It takes some getting used to, but you do get used to it.

---

* Please note the word 'world'. For Europe, English is not such a bad choice. With its part Germanic, part Romance ancestry and a modest admixture of Greek, it may well be the right mongrel for the job (though the Slavs beg to differ). And now that most Europeans are exposed to English-language pop music from the womb onwards, there's no serious competition.

The same cannot be said of the main factor that makes English unpronounceable for much of the world's population: its vowels. (There are other problems, too: consonant clusters as in _straw_ and _prompts,_ the lispy sounds of _they_ and _thin_ and the eccentric behaviour of English _r_'s. But let's leave those aside.) The main nuisance about English vowels is that there are so many of them. If you're British, you'll agree that the vowels following the _p_ are different in each item of this list: _par, pear, peer, pipe, poor, power, purr, pull, poop, puke, pin, pan, pain, pen, pawn, pun, point, posh, pose, parade._ That makes twenty different vowels (including the so-called gliding ones, such as _oi_ and the long _i_ and _u_). Now, imagine that your mother tongue had only a handful of them. If you were a Quechua from the Andes or an Inuit from the North American Arctic, it would have only three, and if your first language were Spanish, the number would still be as low as five. Speakers of these languages face double trouble: their mouths are unaccustomed to producing the many vowel sounds of English and their ears are unable to tell them apart. Or to put it more accurately: it's their adult brains that can't cope with the variety. (Children take it in their stride, of course.)

Given good teaching methods and loads of practice, many Quechuas, Inuit, Spaniards and others will eventually master English pronunciation. But whereas Chinese tones are helpfully similar to something we're in the habit of paying attention to, namely intonation, no such aid to the needy is available for English vowels.

And now on to the second similarity between English and Chinese, which is to do with writing. In both languages, words on the page reveal little about what they are going to sound like. Chinese script is deeply unhelpful in this respect: the characters you see contain few if any clues as to which sounds they represent. There's nothing for it but to learn by heart what each character sounds like and what each word looks like. English

The 'gh' in laugh= 'f'
The 'o' in women= 'i'
The 'ti' in motion= 'sh'
GHOTI = 'fish'

'GHOTI' IS A FAVOURITE OF ENGLISH SPELLING REFORMERS. IT COULD BE
PRONOUNCED 'FISH', AS ABOVE. OR IT COULD BE SILENT, AS IN THE GH IN
OUGHT, THE O IN LEOPARD, THE T IN CASTLE AND THE I IN JUICE. FISH, OF
COURSE, ARE SILENT TYPES.

doesn't require such prodigious feats of memory, it's true, but the
vagaries of English spelling are worse than unhelpful. If you grew
up speaking English you probably found it hard enough to get
your head around the hundreds of irregularities. Had you learnt
English mostly from books, rather than from speech, the process
would have been much, much more traumatic. To do anything
like justice to the abominations of English spelling would double
the length of this book. Suffice it to point out that, although they
end with the same four letters, none of these words rhymes with
any of the others: *though, rough, cough, through, bough, thorough*.
And why should *womb, comb* and *bomb* sound so unlike? If this
isn't enough to convince you that English spelling is a migraine-
inducer for any foreigner, just get online and Google 'ghoti' (see
above) or 'Chaos by Charivarius'.

   Historically, the regrettable situation in East Asia has come
about in a different way from that in Britain. The Chinese script
has never tried to be phonetically consistent. English speech and

spelling, on the other hand, were on reasonable terms until, many centuries ago, most of the spoken words began to go their own weird way and their inky partners refused to follow. It's been chaos ever since.

Nowadays, however, both languages have more or less the same main reason for not adopting a writing system that more closely mirrors their pronunciation: the speakers disagree among themselves on how to speak. (Adherence to tradition also plays a role, but that can be overcome, in principle at least.) In Chinese, the so-called dialects are really languages in their own right, but since their grammatical structures are as good as identical, the traditional writing system serves them equally well. Speakers of, say, Mandarin from Beijing and Wu from Shanghai will hardly understand each other's speech, but can read each other's writing without much effort. Both use the character 人 for 'person', for instance, but in Beijing it's pronounced 'ren', whereas Shanghai prefers 'nin' – or 'zen' when they want to be posh. In English, the situation is less extreme, in that most speakers can make themselves understood to most others. But given the range of dialects, a spelling reform to satisfy speakers from every region of England, Wales, Scotland, Ireland, Australia, New Zealand, South Africa, Canada and every United State is unthinkable.

If either of the languages ever manages to put an easier, less frustrating writing system into place, it's more likely to be Chinese than English. Now that most Chinese schoolchildren learn to speak Standard Mandarin, the traditional characters could be replaced by *pinyin*, literally 'spelled-out sounds', the system developed in China during the 1950s to render Mandarin in Latin script, closely following its phonology. There is a snag, however. Chinese has a considerable number of identical-sounding words (homophones) that pinyin, unlike character script, cannot distinguish between. This could be remedied, but at the cost of complicating the spelling.

Reading this chapter so far, you may have felt a twinge of indignation. Hey, wait a minute – English isn't *that* tricky. Hasn't English conquered the world because millions and millions of people are happy to learn a language without the genders of French, the cases of German, the conjugations of Spanish and the mutations of Welsh?

Well, we're coming to that. Before I partially concede your point, I must correct one possible misunderstanding: the success of English in conquering a good part of the world is nothing to do with its being easy. Latin conquered many lands, and it was a damn sight more complex than English in terms of gender, case and conjugation. Aramaic, Greek and Arabic, three more languages that made it big at some point in history, were no less grammatically ornate than Latin. Their success was attributable to historical and political factors, not to any supposed linguistic advantages, and the same is true of English. If English is an easier language than those four, that's really just a matter of luck.

And is it really easier? Well – yes, in a way. While the grammar of every language has elusive subtleties and niceties, beginners tend to struggle most with *inflection*: the letters added at the end of a word for grammatical reasons (or, in some languages, at the beginning or even in the middle). Of course, English is not entirely without inflection: *larger*, *largest*, *John's*, *drawing*, *burnt*, *eaten*: all the bold letters represent inflection. Compared to most languages, however, this is a modest set, and its modesty does make English easier for the novice. As it happens, however, Chinese can pride itself on the same asset – even more so than English. So here we encounter the long-awaited third commonality: paucity of inflection. This is the redeeming quality that prevents the two of them from being lousy world languages.

Which is not to say that, for adult language learners, it's plain sailing from here on. Both grammars still have their rough patches and rocky waters. Chinese nouns may not have genders, but the language has dozens of so-called classifiers, and to speak it well, you must know which noun demands which classifier. It's a bit like the English habit of saying 'five head of cattle' and 'three pairs of scissors' rather than the ungrammatical 'five cattles' or 'three scissors'. In Chinese, all nouns behave like this, and it's not always easy to tell whether a noun insists on 'heads', 'pairs' or yet another classifier. (Fortunately, there is one catch-all alternative: pronounced *gè* in Mandarin. It's a word that some native speakers will use when they don't know the correct classifier, and non-natives can get away with using. But stylish it ain't.)

Remember, however, the saying about the mote in the other person's eye and the beam in your own, and be assured that English grammar is as beam-filled as any. The strong verbs, to begin with, such as *befall – befell – befallen* and *read – read – read*, are a definite pain to most adult learners. So is negation: whereas most languages have one clear word, such as *not*, to negate any sentence, English prefers to negate *you write* as *you don't write, you will write* as *you won't write* and you can write as *you can't write* – and please note that the o's in *do* and *don't* and the a's in *can* and *can't* do not sound the same. And there are more oddities. Why does English say 'I want you to listen' rather than the more straightforward 'I want that you listen'? Why do prepositions so often move away from the word they belong to, as in 'this is the girl I'm in love *with*'? Native speakers don't think twice about any of this, but it's all deeply puzzling to a non-native on first encounter. I'm not suggesting, mind you, that English is *more* puzzling than other languages. I just don't want you to come away with the idea that its more humane inflection level makes learning English a piece of cake.

Finally, let's return to numbers, for though they may not be very interesting linguistically, they are hugely consequential in practical terms. English as a world language is not only very much like Chinese, it may also be superseded by it. Quite a few political pundits believe the 'Asian giant' will be the next superpower in economic, political and military terms. If so, it's not impossible that it will also become the next linguistic powerhouse. Since Chinese is in some ways very different from Western languages, this would be bad news for Europeans: learning the new world language would become a more demanding job than it is now. But as we've seen, Chinese is not more difficult than English per se, and many Africans and Asians will actually find it somewhat easier. Much hangs on reform of the script: without the hurdle of its characters, learning Chinese would become a good deal less forbidding for almost everybody.

And what would it mean for Britain if Chinese were to achieve global dominance? Thanks to America, English would no doubt still be a major international language. But in all likelihood, your children or grandchildren would learn Chinese at school. Isn't that a heart-warming prospect, when you think about it? At long last, after many generations of widespread linguistic disability, Britons would become as multilingual as the rest of Europe. Which is good news, because the benefits of bilingualism have in recent years been piling up like laundry. Scientists have found that fluency in more than one language improves your memory, enhances your intelligence, delays the onset of Alzheimer's – the list is growing by the day. So if you want the best for your children and grandchildren, welcome the rise of China.

Further reading

Most chapters in this book are based on a range of sources, both printed and online. Among these, Wikipedia and Wiktionary were often the first in line, though never the last. What makes them particularly useful is their availability in many languages. The Wikipedia and Wiktionary in English are the largest by far, but when it comes to linguistic information, the other ones, from German to Romansh, can be invaluable. I also found the following books particularly inspiring, and they should be of interest to anyone who has enjoyed *Lingo*.

Ti Alkire and Carol Rosen, *Romance Languages*, Cambridge University Press, 2010. Not exactly a holiday page-turner, but a neat presentation of how Latin developed into the 'Big Five' of the Romance family.

David Bellos, *Is That a Fish in Your Ear? Translation and the Meaning of Everything*. Penguin Books, 2011. The only book on translation you ever need to read, unless you want to make it your job. Erudite, recalcitrant and fun.

Guy Deutscher, *The Unfolding of Language*, Arrow, 2006. Deutscher is that rare thing: a linguistic scholar who writes entertainingly. My chapters on Romani and Welsh owe something to this book.

Guy Deutscher, *Through the Language Glass*, Arrow, 2011. Here Deutscher argues, somewhat heretically, that language does shape our thought processes and perception – less than laypeople like to think, but more than linguists tend to give it credit for.

Philip Durkin, *Borrowed Words*, Oxford University Press, 2014. The principal etymologist of the Oxford English Dictionary focuses on English loanwords from the twenty most important source languages.

Nicholas Evans, *Dying Words*, Wiley-Blackwell, 2009. Does it really matter if languages become extinct? Evans might well convince you that we are indeed poorer for every language that dies. He focuses mostly on regions outside Europe, but it has a beautiful section on Avdo Međedović, the twentieth-century 'Homer from Montenegro'.

Bernd Heine and Tania Kuteva, *The Changing Languages of Europe*, Oxford University Press, 2006. Like Alkire and Rosen's book, this is not for the beginner, but those who soldier on will be rewarded with splendid panoramas.

George McLennan, *Scots Gaelic: An Introduction to the Basics* and *A Gaelic Alphabet: A Guide to the Pronunciation of Gaelic Letters and Words*, Argyll Publishing, 2005 and 2009. I disagree with McLennan on one or two points, but these slim books are both informative and well written.

Karl Menninger, *Number Words and Number Symbols*, MIT, 1969. While riddled with outdated ideas, this is also a treasure trove of curious information. The chapter on Breton was born out of it.

Nicholas Ostler, *Empires of the Word*, HarperCollins, 2005. A monumental work that makes good on its subtitle – 'A language history of the world'. Five years later, Ostler published *The Last Lingua Franca*, about dominant languages, with English as the latest in the sequence.

Acknowledgements

Among the chapters that for various reasons did not make the leap from my Dutch book *Taaltoerisme* ('Language Tourism') into *Lingo*, one was about the meanings of family names. It argued that names originating in unfamiliar languages are harder to remember, with the unfortunate consequence that we, as humans, experience less sympathy for the people so named. As a remedy – generally impracticable, but theoretically effective – I suggested that writers and editors translate these unfamiliar family names, so as to bring them closer to the reader's heart.

In the following paragraphs, dozens of people from all over Europe will be thanked for their support in the making of this book. Most of their names are not of English origin, and there's a risk that the reader will gloss over them and register no more than a fleeting sensation of strangeness. Therefore, I will take a leaf out of my own book and give approximate translations, insofar as I've been able to figure their meaning out.

First and foremost, there's my wife, Marleen Bekker, who deserves big thanks for her wisdom, her consistent support and her mixture of wit and silliness. Also, she is not particularly interested in language, which may be one of the reasons why I love her. Her last name is the word (in Low Saxon, not Dutch) for 'baker', so in English it would be Baker or Baxter.

A few chapters were originally written by friends. For the chapter on Manx, credit is due to my irresistibly grumbly social-media pal, the Isle of Man based translator Frauke Watson. The stories about Cornish, Finnish and Maltese were authored by my dear real-life friend, the linguist Jenny Audring, who also turns up in the chapter on Dutch. Jenny's last name derives from the name of a village in Latvia, whose etymology is obscure.

Expert comments, inspiration and friendly help were provided by Richard Bank (sign languages), Marion de Groot (Chinese), Casper de Jonge (Italian), Robert de Kock (Basque), Benjamin den Butter (Turkish), Finnur Friðriksson (Icelandic), Charlotte Gooskens (Icelandic), Cornelius Hasselblatt (Sami), Axel Holvoet (Latvian), Franka Hummels (Belarusian), Geraint Jennings (Channel Island Norman), Yoma Jonker (sign languages), John Kirk (Shelta), Matej Klemen (Slovene), Ihar Klimau (Belarusian), Katy McMillan (Scots), Yaron Matras (Anglo-Romani and Shelta), Joachim Matzinger (Albanian), Astrid Menz (Gagauz), Brian Ó Broin (Irish), Colm Ó Broin (Irish), Pekka Sammallahti (Sami), Hotimir Tivadar (Slovene), Tereza Trefilíková (Czech), Mario van de Visser (Basque), Duco van Dijk (Portuguese), Jan van Tuin (Italian) and Leandra Zoulfoukaridis (Greek).

Some of their surnames are easily translatable: de Groot corresponds to Long or Longman, de Jonge to Young, de Cock to Cook, den Butter refers to the same craft as Tinker, Friðriksson means 'Frederick's son', Jonker has a meaning similar to Duke or Knight, Klemen is a form of the first name Clement, Klimau is 'Clement's son', Ó Broin means 'descendant of Bran', Sammallahti means 'moss bay', Tivadar is the Hungarian form of Theodore, van de Visser corresponds to Fisher, van Dijk to Dyke and van Tuin to Towne or Garden. A particularly interesting case is Zoulfoukaridis, which means 'descendant of Zoulfoukar', a man's name inspired by the name of Mohammad's sword.

Many chapters benefited greatly from the comments provided by readers Trix Clerx, Mirjam Jochemsen, Rutger Kiezebrink, Niala Maharaj, Liesbeth Tettero, Piet Vermeer and Tom Wijns. Of these, Niala – journalist, novelist and long-time friend – deserves special mention, as she introduced me to the wonders of the English language (whereas I failed miserably at introducing her to the wonders of Dutch). Clerx translates as Clarkson, Maharaj as King and Vermeer as Lake; Jochemsen means 'Joachim's son'.

To Scriptum, the publishers of *Taaltoerisme*, I'm grateful for their generosity, for the freedom they allow their authors and for their implicit trust, which invites trust. No written contract was signed, but Scriptum have proved to be as good as their word.

I'm also indebted to Caroline Dawnay of United Agents, who is an incredible agent: experienced, kind and amazingly effective. With her assistant Sophie Scard, they make a dream team.

Profile Books welcomed me warmly, have consistently believed in the book, and have brought their professionalism to bear on it. Thank you, Andrew Franklin, Mark Ellingham and Sarah Hull, and for proofreading, indexing and design, their team of Susanne Hillen, Diana LeCore and Henry Iles. Getting from *Taaltoerisme* to *Lingo* was a memorable process which has taught me a thing or two. The name LeCore is bound to derive from Norman French for 'the heart'.

Translator, linguist and columnist Alison Edwards had what it took to reproduce the substance and the tone of the Dutch book into English: expertise, stylistic flair and the patience to deal with a demanding author. Working with her was a delight. Also, I'm obliged to the Dutch Foundation for Literature (Letterenfonds) for funding her work. The book in its ultimate form, however, owes a huge debt to the work of novelist Jonathan Buckley. A hawk-eyed, patient and erudite editor, he has an enviable command of the English language. I'm honoured he agreed to be on the team.

A few of the people mentioned above have moreover published books that were of great importance for *Lingo*. The chapter about Dutch was based on Jenny Audring's 2010 PhD thesis about the 'reinvention', as she terms it, of the Dutch pronoun; it can be downloaded at *http://tinyurl.com/AudringPhD*. Finnur Friðriksson's 2008 PhD thesis about the stability of Icelandic (*http://tinyurl. com/FridhrikssonPhD*) provided much-needed information for the chapter about his mother tongue. And *Travellers and their language*, edited by John M. Kirk and Dónall Ó Baoill (Queen's University Belfast, 2002) proved of great use for understanding what Shelta is, and what it isn't. Of course, hundreds of other sources have been consulted to write *Lingo*. I have listed a few that may be of interest for a general readership in the 'Further reading' section.

In spite of all the support received and sources consulted, mistakes are bound to show up in this book. As always, criticism should be directed at me, the author. Should my response to it appear a bit prickly, please don't take it personally. It's just that my own family name means 'thorn'.

Photo credits

Images in this book have been assembled from my own collections, from friends and associates, Wikipedia, flickr and other online resources. I have endeavoured to credit all sources and photographers; apologies to anyone who is not properly credited – omissions can be corrected in future editions.

17 Europa Polyglotta map by Gottfried Hensel (1741).

22 Lenguas finougrias (Wikipedia).

26 Matterhorn sign: Kecko/flickr.

30 Napoleon statue by Eugène Guillaume/Fondation Napoléon

38 Bucharest statue: Dennis Jarvis/flickr.

41 South Ossetia crest: Wikipedia.

47 Paide castle: Ivo Kruusamägi Wikipedia.

51 Iberian blinds: Gaston Dorren.

55 Hans Christian Andersen statue: Carlos Delgado/Wikipedia.

60 Guernésiaise: Man vyi/flickr.

65 Yiddish demonstration: Kheel Center, Cornell University.

69 Saga: Luc Van Braekel/flickr.

77 Utepils: Aslak Raanes/flickr.

83 Vill Gaer: Marco Galasso/flickr.

87 Frisian Gay Pride Parade: flickr.

92 Olof Palme: SPÖ Press/flickr.

98 Camp Nou Stadium: Wikipedia.

103 Minefield: NH53/flickr.

108 Snobordový Klub: Gaston Dorren.

113 Szczęsny: arsenal.com.

118 Oi Polloi: GothEric/flickr.

123 Anna Karenina first edition.

132 Cartoon By Inussik/Inuscomix

142 Romani wagon: National Library of Ireland/Wikipedia.

150 Sappho And Alcaeus by Lawrence Alma-Tadema: Walters Art Museum/Wikimedia.

153 Chegadas: Kyller Costa Gorgônio/flickr.

163 Gina Lollobrigida: Wikimedia.

170 Menhirs: David Barrena/flickr.

176 Doutzen Kroes: fervent-adepte-de-la-mode/flickr.

181 Django Reinhardt: William P. Gottlieb/US Library of Congress.

191 Byrgyrs: Moshe Reuveni/flickr.

201 Ukrainian sign: Eamon Curry/flickr.

211 Gaeltacht: Sludge G/flickr.

221 High Tide: David Merrett/flickr.

241 Great Dictator: Wikipedia.

257 No X In Finnish: Juan Freire/flickr.

269 Armenian monument: Nina Stössinger/flickr.

273 Hungarian Language Museum: www.nyelvmuzeum.hu

276 Valletta harbour: www.maltaholidays.uk

281 'Ghoti': www.iridium77.livejournal.com

Index

Figures in **bold** indicate main references; those in *italics* refer to captions.

D

M